Wiki Works

Wiki Works

Teaching Web Research and Digital Literacy in History and Humanities Classrooms

Robert W. Maloy and Allison Malinowski

ROWMAN & LITTLEFIELD
Lanham • Boulder • New York • London

Published by Rowman & Littlefield
A wholly owned subsidiary of The Rowman & Littlefield Publishing Group, Inc.
4501 Forbes Boulevard, Suite 200, Lanham, Maryland 20706
www.rowman.com

Unit A, Whitacre Mews, 26–34 Stannary Street, London SE11 4AB

British Library Cataloguing in Publication Information Available

Library of Congress Cataloging-in-Publication Data Is Available

ISBN 978-1-4758-3236-5 (cloth: alk. paper)
ISBN 978-1-4758-3237-2 (pbk: alk. paper)
ISBN 978-1-4758-3242-6 (electronic)

♾™ The paper used in this publication meets the minimum requirements of American National Standard for Information Sciences—Permanence of Paper for Printed Library Materials, ANSI/NISO Z39.48–1992.

Printed in the United States of America

Contents

Preface

Wiki Works: Teaching Web Research and Digital Literacy in the History and Humanities Classrooms is a book about how students and teachers—together as learning partners—can use interactive wiki technologies to transform how history and humanities education is experienced in K–12 schools.

Wikis, online sites that emerge from the contributions of multiple authors, teach students academic content, web research skills, and the importance of collaborative thinking while showing how to *access* and *assess* online information—the foundations of digital literacy in today's Internet interconnected world. As classroom learning activities, constructing wiki pages is a way to change instructional practices from adult-centered presentations to student-driven inquiries and explorations as frameworks for academic learning. As tools for addressing academic standards and curriculum, wikis engage and motivate students through multimodal and multicultural learning experiences.

The very first wiki appeared in March 1995, launched by inventor and computer programmer Ward Cunningham, who called this new software the WikiWikiWeb. He chose "wiki" from the Hawaiian language word meaning "quick" inspired by his experience using a Honolulu airport cab service called the Wiki Wiki Shuttle.

A wiki is a type of "collaborative software" that enables quick and easy changes by a group of creators, Cunningham explained in an interview many years later. "I made it on the web and allowed people to come to a website and create something" (quoted in Grigas, 2014). Cunningham's intention for that first wiki was to dynamically "link together" the employees of his Portland, Oregon, technology company so they could build on each other's ideas and "discover the pattern language of programming."

He also had two other more expansive goals in mind. First, he wanted to get people talking with each other, "to stroke that story-telling nature in all of us."

Second, and for Cunningham, "perhaps most important, I wanted people who wouldn't normally author to find it comfortable authoring" so others could discover and learn from what they had to say (quoted in Venners, 2003).

"The appeal of wiki technology lies in the act of rethinking the familiar," concluded a group of information scientists in their book, *Wiki: Web Collaboration* (Ebersbach et al., 2008, p. 24). Rethinking is possible, in part, because wiki technology is open access and simple to use, allowing "virtually anyone to completely edit pages without difficulty." Moreover, any user can "contribute significantly to the structure of the site by simply creating new links and adding new pages" (Ebersbach et al., 2008, p. 11). In schools, rethinking occurs as teachers and students implement new ways of learning using technology in the history and humanities curriculum.

Our story about wikis and new ways of exploring technology's potentials is embedded in twelve years of developing wikis to deliver content in teacher education courses in the College of Education at the University of Massachusetts Amherst. The first of these, *resourcesforhistoryteachers*, a standards-based, open content wiki, has evolved from a narrowly conceived site containing online materials for students in one college course to a widely expanding digital resource with more than 800 pages and thousands of links used daily by students and teachers from all over the world.

Visit the *resourcesforhistoryteachers* wiki:
https://resourcesforhistoryteachers.wikispaces.com/home

---

resourcesforhistoryteachers displays a page for each of the learning standards in the Massachusetts K–12 History & Social Science Curriculum Framework as well as the national Advanced Placement (AP) standards for world history, U.S. history, government and politics, and art history. Newly developed individual pages focus on dramatic events, historical biographies, influential literature, special curricular topics, and democratic teaching methods, all of which are explored in the book's chapters with strategies for transforming curriculum and promoting learning by engaging students, supporting teachers, and differentiating classroom instruction.

resourcesforhistoryteachers has provided ideas for developing other curricular wikis: *Teaching Resources for English* focusing on world and American literature along with young adult books and writing strategies taught in English/language arts classrooms; *Teaching Geography* presenting resources for learning about people and places around the world; and *TEAMS-Tutoring in Schools* serving as the free online "tech book" for a flipped learning college undergraduate course.

Visit *Teaching Resources for English* here:
https://teachingresourcesforenglish.wikispaces.com/Welcome+
to+the+Wiki
Visit *TEAMS-Tutoring in Schools* here:
https://teams-tutoringinschools.wikispaces.com
Visit *Teaching Geography* here:
https://teachinggeography.wikispaces.com/home

Each wiki contributes to the story told in this book, as do the efforts of students and teachers accessing the pages and contributing content to the sites. Since 2006, more than 200 college students in courses taught by Robert Maloy have edited and expanded pages for *resourcesforhistoryteachers*. Many of these college students have become teachers who now use wikis for planning and teaching curricular to elementary, middle, and high school students. In addition, educators in the United States and from around the world access these wikis and post resources, too. Members of the New England World History Teachers Association have added to the *AP World History* pages, and middle and high school students have contributed to pages as part of class learning activities.

As authors of this book, each of us is old enough to remember teaching and learning before the arrival of computers. We now find ourselves occupying dual spaces as participants in and researchers of education's ongoing digital revolution. We have seen how interactive technologies like wikis can create engaging educational environments for personalized learning, student-centered instruction, and collaborative and project-based activities (Center for Digital Education & National School Boards Association, 2015). We agree with researchers from Project Tomorrow (2016, p. 2), who, after surveying students, educators, and community members throughout the country, concluded that "new technological advancements and resulting disruptive innovations" will continue changing the roles of students and teachers in ways both "evolutionary and advantageous."

When *resourcesforhistoryteachers* began in 2006, wikis were one of many new digital technologies competing for the attention of educators along with blogs, teacher-made websites, audience response systems, social bookmarking services, podcasting, screen and lecture captures, online homework systems, social media outlets like Facebook and Skype, and more. At the time, we had only vague notions of how these new technologies could impact school curriculum and instructional practices.

Initially, wikis were hailed as potent tools for teaching and learning. In one of its first "7 Things You Should Know About" briefs about technology trends, the Educause Learning Initiative (2005) defined wikis as a "database created by a group rather than an individual," resulting in "surprisingly robust, open-ended, collaborative group sites." Since they could function as a "composition system, a discussion medium, a repository, a mail system, and a tool for collaboration," wikis were open to many different imaginative and creative uses. Answering the question, "Where is it going?" the Educause editors declared, "Since wikis are easy to edit, they carry an inherent potential to change how we construct knowledge repositories on the Web."

To date, however, wikis have not emerged as a widely used educational technology in schools, and there are important systemic reasons why this has been the case. Wikis reside on the intersection between the practices of the past and possibilities of the future, and, as Alan Collins and Richard Halverson (2009, p. 6) noted nearly a decade ago, "There are deep incompatibilities between the demands of the new technologies and the traditional school."

Given their collaborative and interactive design, wikis invite adults and students to redefine long-standing patterns of teacher-centered instruction by flattening the roles of learner and teacher through a "partnering pedagogy" (Prensky, 2010). Making such changes is not easy to do in schools where teachers, in Larry Cuban's (2008) succinct phrase, find themselves "hugging the middle" between student-centered approaches to learning and adult-directed instructional methods as they struggle to address mandated learning standards while raising student achievement scores.

In this context, wikis answer a question about the digital revolution first posted nearly two decades ago: "The Web may be a great way to distribute information, but can you really *teach* with it?" (Foshay & Bergeron, 2000, p. 16). Our answer is resoundingly "Yes!" Educators can teach with wikis when they collaborate with students to create learning experiences that fully utilize the interactive and collaborative nature of digital technologies.

In each chapter, we present what we have learned about using wikis to change existing instructional practices, promote student learning, and transform history and humanities education across grade levels. Those lessons involve students and teachers working collaboratively to build and use wiki pages that support inquiry-based, multimedia, multicultural, and student-centered learning. We begin by locating wikis within the digital-to-print revolution under way in education today. Then we show how wikis can address curriculum standards (chapter 2); teach digital literacy (chapter 3); uncover hidden histories and untold stories (chapter 4); explore dramatic events and special topics (chapter 5); learn about notable people through biographies and books (chapter 6); and engage students through flipped learning (chapter 7).

As we write this book, students and teachers are accessing learning resources in ways never before possible—even a few years ago. With a smartphone, tablet, laptop, or desktop device, for example, anyone can not only read "the original text of the Odyssey . . . but watch a Ted Talk video about its relevancy in today's society and listen to a podcast debate among modern day scholars about the legacy of Greek poems on today's modern songwriting" (Project Tomorrow, 2016, p. 2).

With a wiki, students and teachers can not only access multiple resources but also assemble and curate classroom and curriculum-specific collections of resources about Greek literature—or any history or humanities topic—in one online location and use those materials to change how teachers teach and students learn. On *The Iliad and The Odyssey* page on the *Teaching Resources for English* wiki, for example, there are not only links to the full text of the poems but also to an online biography of Homer from the American Academy of Poets, a *National Geographic* magazine article about whether or not any single author wrote the poems, a beginner's guide to the Trojan War assembled by an anthropology professor at the University of California San Diego, and teaching resources collected by the *New York Times'* Learning Network.

Visit *The Iliad and The Odyssey* Page:
https://teachingresourcesforenglish.wikispaces.com/The+Iliad+and+The+Odyssey

---

Assembling wiki-based multimodal collections that combine text, pictures, audio, and video materials gives students and teachers a collage of resources to investigate and cross-check rather than providing them with a single source to read and remember. That has been the goal of *resourcesforhistoryteachers* and its sister wiki projects. Students and teachers can do the same by building their own educational wikis. To fulfill such goal, everyone needs strategies, approaches, and examples to guide their work as learning partners. You will find those ideas in the pages ahead. We hope you will find *Wiki Works* an ongoing resource for successful teaching and learning with technology.

Acknowledgments

We would like to thank the following individuals for their ideas and inspirations in the writing of this book: Sharon A. Edwards, Bryan Malinowski, Irene S. LaRoche, Torrey Trust, Sinead Meaney, Lexie Brearley, Jessica Charnley, Katerina Sherrick, Samantha Whitman, Brian Pastore, Ryan Walsh, Jeff Whitney, Haley Clark, Jeremy Greene, Joe Emery, Kate Curtin, Kaelan Burkett, Amanda Dente, Eric Ziemba, Helen van Riel, and students from courses taught at the University of Massachusetts Amherst, Chelmsford High School, Shrewsbury Middle School, Amherst Regional Middle School, and the Williston Northampton School. We also want to thank our editor, Sarah Jubar, who believed in this project from the beginning and has provided the guidance to make this book better.

Chapter 1

From Print to Digital

The New England Primer—the most widely used educational textbook in colonial America—was first published in Boston in 1690. For more than 300 years since then, going to school in this country can be said to have had three constant elements: paper books, a teacher, and a chalkboard (Reynolds, 1976). Today, with the availability and affordability of Internet-accessible laptops, tablets, and smartphones—coupled with the high costs of textbooks and other educational materials—educators are organizing more and more school learning around the use of digital resources, interactive websites, and computer-based tools and apps.

The print-to-digital transition in schools has reached dramatic proportions. There is now one computer for every five students in the nation's public schools (Education Week, 2015). In one national survey, a large majority of K–12 school technology leaders (84 percent) said they expect instructional materials to be at least 50 percent digital within the next three years. Survey respondents said open educational resources were in use in more than half of the districts while half of the districts said they were implementing one-to-one laptop and tablet computer initiatives for students (Center for Digital Education, 2016). Forty percent of schools were offering online classes for students (Blackboard, 2016).

Bring Your Own Device (BYOD) programs are expanding rapidly—14 percent of IT leaders report they are fully engaged in implementing these initiatives, while another 56 percent said they are planning to implement a program in their district (Consortium for School Networking, 2015, p. 17). Just over four out of five (82 percent) of educational administrators responding to the 2015 national Speak Up survey said their schools are using digital content and online resources in the classroom; one in four rated their level of paperless-ness at 50 percent and increasing (Project Tomorrow, 2016, p. 4).

While the paper-to-digital shift is far from total—paper books are not disappearing from schools anytime soon—online resources and multimedia materials in e-text formats invite new instructional practices. They also raise issues and challenges for understanding technology's impacts on teaching and learning, including how digital materials have become integral parts of curriculum and instruction, how students are using technology for personal learning in and outside the classroom, and the ways that teacher- and student-made wikis can function as interactive, collaboratively built resources in history and humanities classrooms.

READING IN A DIGITAL WORLD

The book has been the "world's most important form of written record" for more than a thousand years, notes writer Keith Houston (2016), and it is once again at the center of dramatic changes in human culture. As Houston explains, "Just as paper superseded parchment, movable type put scribes out of a job, and the codex, or printed book, overtook the papyrus scroll." Electronic books are dramatically altering our relationship with physical books and the information they contain.

There are millions of books now "available in electronic form" and accessible on a variety of Internet-accessible handheld and mobile devices as well as stationary desktop computers (Baron, 2015, p. 5). Called e-books or digital books, there are two basic types—a digital version of a print original and what linguistic professor Naomi Baron refers to as a "digitally native" text that was specifically designed to make use of the interactive capabilities of computer technology and Internet access. Digital native books enable readers to manipulate images and text on the screen, access live links to Internet sites and embedded videos, take quizzes and receive feedback online, and use search and glossary functions to move seamlessly within the text to locate information about topics.

Tracing shifts in people's reading habits from print to digital, Baron (2015, p. x) cites three important milestones: the arrival of Amazon's Kindle e-reader in 2007, the launch of Apple iPad in 2010, and the continuing improvements in smartphone functionality that make it easier and easier to text on small screens. Each development has made it possible for people of all ages to comfortably access information in digital formats.

Americans have become "hybrid consumers" of printed books and digital texts, concluded the Pew Research Center (Perrin, 2016a, 2016b; Rainie & Perrin, 2015). Seven in ten (72 percent) adults said they read a book in any format during the past year—63 percent reported reading a printed copy. After a period of dramatic growth, e-book and audiobook readership settled to about 20 percent (for e-books) and 12 percent (for audiobooks). Young adults (eighteen to twenty-nine years old), women, and people with higher levels of education and income read more in both print and e-book formats. In part because they are still in school, those aged below thirty years read the most books (69 percent read print books and 34 percent read e-texts).

Reading is the process of making meaning from text, and school-age students access enormous amounts of digital text every day, expanding the meaning of how reading happens (Guernsey & Levine, 2015). Virtually everyone below thirty years uses the Internet (98 percent), has a cell phone (96 percent; with 77 percent having a smartphone), and logs on to social networking sites (90 percent). One in three younger Americans use Twitter, and the use of Snapchat, Instagram, and other social media sites is growing steadily (Zickuhr & Rainie, 2014).

Interacting through social media is a dominant feature of daily life for young people today. A report from the consumer watchdog organization Common Sense Media (2015) found that teens spend on average nine hours a day and tweens spend six hours a day using entertainment media, apart from media use at school. Much of this media involvement happens through multi-tasking when youngsters are texting while playing online games or watching television while doing schoolwork. Television and listening to music, so called old media because they have been available the longest, remain the most popular forms of entertainment for teens and tweens, although these materials are increasingly being consumed in new ways through phones, tablets, or other mobile devices.

The Common Sense Media researchers (2015) found gender, income, and group differences in their survey data. Boys spend more time playing video games, while girls use social media. Low-income adolescents have significantly less access to the latest and most powerful computers, tablets, and smartphones, limiting their use of these tools. African American youth spend more time with media than white or Hispanic youth. Among all groups, 39 percent of digital screen time was spent in passive consumption (listening and watching), 25 percent using interactive content (playing games), 26 percent communicating with others (using social media to share information), and just 3 percent in creating content (writing, coding, or making digital music or art).

STUDENTS, TECHNOLOGY, AND LEARNING

Digital technologies are transforming the learning experiences of students and not just because schools have many computers in classrooms. Rather, change is happening in the ways that digital devices and online materials are being used across the grade levels—in and outside of school. Project

Tomorrow (2016) reports that 46 percent of high school students are using online textbooks, 68 percent of teachers are incorporating videos from the Internet into classroom instruction, and 80 percent of principals believe that technology increases student engagement in education and learning.

K–12 students, meanwhile, increasingly "exhibit *free agent learning* behaviors where they are tapping into digital tools to explore academic interests" (Project Tomorrow, 2016, p. 10). "The New Digital Playbook," a report based on Project Tomorrow's (2014) research on 9,000 schools nationwide, drew a distinction between "teacher-facilitated" and "student-initiated" technology use. In "teacher-facilitated" situations, adults establish the framework for students' technology use. Nearly 70 percent of students access class information through a teacher or school website, blog, or learning management system; about half of the students at all grade levels take tests online; about one in three middle and high schoolers use online textbooks; and about one in four watches teacher-created videos as part of class assignments.

By contrast, student-initiated use contradicts a popular view that students access technology outside of school mainly for entertainment and recreation. In student-initiated contexts, young learners choose different ways for technology to support academic learning, including texting with classmates about schoolwork, taking photos of assignments with mobile devices, locating online videos to help with homework, collaborating with peers on social media to complete projects, and chatting online about academic topics. YouTube, Snapchat, and Instagram are the most widely used social networks; Twitter and Facebook are the least used (Speaking of Tomorrow, 2016).

Writing and reading with digital tools are also core elements of student-initiated technology use. High school students who consider themselves advanced computer users report spending fourteen hours a week using technology for writing ranging from essays and reports (75 percent for girls; 60 percent for boys) to e-mail, creative writing, journaling, poetry, blogging, and tweeting. Fourteen percent of girls and twenty percent of boys do coding. When reading, middle school students report they prefer "to read digital materials rather than printed materials, and 51 percent believe that online textbooks should be an essential component within future schools" (Project Tomorrow, 2015, p. 6).

Members of a media generation who have never known a world without computers, the Internet, mobile phones, and other technologies, today's students, "want greater alignment between their out of school learning and their in-school learning." Across grade levels, genders, and communities, students express a "common vision for the future" where all students in school have "greater access to online sites, use of mobile devices and social media" and have "digital tools that help them to facilitate collaboration, communications and self-organization." Today's students believe that having a personal mobile device, playing digital games, and doing text messaging at school are the best ways to create "un-tethered learning experiences that are rich in interactive digital content" (Project Tomorrow, 2015, pp. 11–13).

After surveying thirteen- to eighteen-year-old students in forty-nine states, the national retailer Barnes & Noble College (2016) also found technology integral to how they want to learn—at school and in their families and communities. At school, younger and older teens overwhelmingly prefer to "learn by doing" through class discussions, working out problems, and receiving individual attention from teachers. For these youngsters, learning by listening was rated their least beneficial way to learn.

Technology, the students told the researchers, is at the center of what they want from school. As learners, they want to be "challenged, they want to be empowered to make their own decisions, and as digital natives, they expect technology to play an instrumental role in their educational experience" (Barnes & Noble College, 2016, p. 8). They find smartboards, do-it-yourself learning, digital textbooks, websites with study materials, online videos, game-based learning systems, and social media/user-generated content especially helpful to them educationally.

TECHNOLOGY'S IMPACT DEPENDS ON ITS USE

Teachers, in general, see technology as being helpful personally, professionally, and instructionally. In one survey, 92 percent of teachers said technology made their teaching more effective (Schaffhauser & Nagel, 2016). Teachers also believe that integrating computers and other digital tools as part of daily lessons motivates students to learn while promoting positive attitudes, behaviors, and skills. But many teachers are less certain that technology results in higher achievement in academic subjects as measured by standardized test scores (Pressey, 2013).

Educators involved in Advanced Placement (AP) programs or the National Writing Project (NWP)—individuals who tend to be more highly technologically skilled than most of their colleagues—have strong, positive attitudes about technology's impact on them as professionals (Purcell et al., 2013). Virtually everyone surveyed (92 percent) said the Internet has had a "major impact" on their ability to locate information and resources for daily lessons. Most commonly, AP/NWP teachers ask students to research online and to access and submit assignments digitally. However, only a small number have students engage in discussions online, develop blogs and wikis, or access collaborative learning platforms to edit writing or accomplish group projects.

Despite the favorable rating given to computers and digital tools by many educators, technology has not changed long-standing patterns of teacher-centered instruction in classrooms (Cuban, 2013, 2016; Education Week, 2015, 2016). Summarizing the results of *Education Week* magazine's yearly Technology Counts survey, one staff writer noted that in most schools, "a handful of 'early adopters' embrace innovative uses of new technology, while their colleagues make incremental or no changes to what they already do" (Herold, 2015). Teachers mainly utilize technology for record keeping, grading, and professional communication and to deliver academic content through PowerPoint presentations and video, while students in their classes are more likely to "use technology daily for drills and review than for project-based or collaborative assignments" (Rebora, 2016).

Educators disagree about technology's impact on student learning. There are studies showing that technology supports student learning gains in literacy development, language acquisition, reading comprehension, motivation to learn, and development of individual self-esteem (O'Hara & Pritchard, 2014). There are other studies that conclude technology use has not resulted in learning gains for students (Ritchel, 2012). Some psychologists warn digital devices are rewiring young brains in ways that reduce attention spans and limit students' willingness to complete challenging tasks (Carr, 2011; Greenfield, 2015). From the opposite perspective, other psychologists see technology as enhancing critical thinking and analytical reasoning (Gee, 2013; Miller, 2014).

In a large-scale international study involving sixty-four countries, the Organization for Economic Cooperation and Development (OECD) found that digital technologies have not been widely adopted in educational systems, but "where they are used in the classroom, their impact on student performance is mixed, at best" (OECD, 2015, p. 15). Looking at the cross-national data, researchers found "no appreciable improvements in student achievement in reading, mathematics or science in the countries that had invested heavily in ICT for education." Moderate computers users did show some gains over students who rarely used technology, but frequent computer users "do a lot worse in most learning outcomes, even after accounting for social background and student demographics" (Schleicher, 2015).

Rather than discount technology's capacity to impact student learning, OECD Education director Andreas Schleicher (2015) offered clarifying thoughts about the findings. He cited the importance of teachers working with students as a key to learning success, noting that "building deep, conceptual understanding and higher order thinking requires intensive teacher-student interactions, and technology sometimes distracts from this valuable human engagement."

Schleicher also cited the need to utilize new technologies in new ways because "adding 21st century technologies to 20th century teaching practices will just dilute the effectiveness of teaching." Technology, said Schleicher, cannot replace poor teaching, but it can "amplify great teaching" while supporting "new pedagogies that focus on learners as active participants."

Other researchers have also found that the way technology is integrated determines its impact on students and learning. In a meta-analysis of ninety-six studies of one-to-one laptop programs around the world between 2001 and 2015, one research team found technology did improve students' test scores in science, writing, math, and English (Zheng et al., 2016). Technology-using students also demonstrated significant gains as writers—writing more often in more genres, revising and editing their work more frequently, and sharing what they had written with many different audiences. But not all one-to-one programs were successful. Programs that gave computers to students without advanced planning and changing the in-class instructional approaches of teachers did not achieve positive outcomes.

In another example, after reviewing dozens of research studies on technology and learning, Linda Darling-Hammond and two other Stanford University researchers concluded that at-risk students "can make substantial gains in learning and technological readiness" when given access to thoughtfully used digital technology (Darling-Hammond, Zielezinski, & Goldman, 2014, p. 4). What at-risk students need, said the Stanford researchers, is access to technology "designed to promote high levels of interactivity and engagement with data and information in multiple forms" (Darling-Hammond, Zielezinski, & Goldman, 2014, p. 15).

The Stanford University research team was clear in stating that having computers mainly present information to students, who then practice problems and answer questions, did not improve academic outcomes. They proposed the following ways to technology to generate improved learning outcomes for students. First, utilize interactive and adaptive learning systems that adjust content and feedback to the needs of individual learners. Second, let students "explore and create" with technology by building websites, creating PowerPoint presentations and video productions, engaging in digital storytelling, and doing other creative self-expression projects. Third, allow students to collaboratively work with adults as well as computers on academic assignments and activities (Darling-Hammond, Zielezinski, & Goldman, 2014, p. 6).

A broad consensus seems to be emerging to achieve substantive and lasting gains in student learning; digital technologies need to be used in ways that feature collaboration, interactivity, and student-initiated/teacher-supported learning. Rather than learning *from* computers, students and teachers need to be learning *with* highly interactive digital technologies. To do so requires understanding each new technology in depth to realize its full potentials for transforming teaching and learning in schools. Given its potential as a collaborative learning tool, wikis are one of those powerful new, highly interactive technologies.

WIKIS—A HIGHLY INTERACTIVE DIGITAL TECHNOLOGY

Since Ward Cunningham's first site in 1995 wikis have been created by businesses, corporations, government agencies, political groups, and individuals to share information, conduct projects, and engage customers and clients (Collins, 2010; Cummings & Barton, 2008; Notari et al., 2016; Noveck, 2010; Richardson, 2010; Seo, 2013). Wikispaces.com, one of the primary wiki site providers, has over ten million registered educator and student users worldwide; PBworks, another company specializing in collaborative software products, has four million people users every month. WikiIndex, a site devoted to tracking wikis online, has over 20,000 pages listing wikis in many fields.

Then there is Wikipedia, a site that, in the words of media researcher Andrew Lih (2009, p. 3), has "singlehandedly invigorated and disrupted the world of encyclopedias, eclipsing nearly every established tome in every language in the world." With over thirty-eight million pages in its English language edition alone, and still growing, Wikipedia has "become the first destination of choice for many and now serves as an integral part of the Internet's fabric of knowledge" (Lih, 2009, p. 4).

Wikipedia is part of a group of sister wiki projects sponsored by the Wikimedia Foundation whose goal is to continue to expand the reach of "user-generated content"—Wikimedia Commons (images, sounds, and video), Wikispecies (life forms dictionary), Wikivoyage (worldwide travel guide), Wikiquote (quotations), Wikinews (open content news), Wikibooks (open content textbooks), Wikiversity (teaching and learning resources), Wikisource (free content library), Wiktionary (dictionary and thesaurus), Wikidata (data), and Metawiki (coordination of wiki development).

Wikis are also found in thousands of K–12 schools where their highly interactive and collaborative design invites teachers and students to create engaging instructional approaches to learning. In 2012, Harvard University researchers identified some 180,000 publicly available educational wikis hosted by the wiki site provider, PBworks (Reich, Murnane, & Willett, 2012). The website *Educational Wikis*, itself a wiki, lists hundreds of school-, teacher-, and classroom-based sites. Wikispaces offers free accounts to educators, further contributing to an ever-growing number of new wiki sites.

Wikis have the potential to promote collaborative and constructivist learning in schools. Anyone can read the content on a public wiki, but members of such a site can add to or revise the material. To make a change to an existing page or create a new one, a member clicks "edit" and enters the new material. The page is now live with the new material in place. Readers can also see all the earlier versions of the page in reverse chronological order by looking in the page history section. Each change is attributed to the member making the change so content does not appear anonymously on the site. Readers can also post comments, suggestions, and ideas for revisions in the discussion section of each page (Barbey, 2009). The entire wiki building process develops design-based thinking, Internet and media literacy, and new patterns of web communication for adults and younger learners alike.

In schools, wikis create digital interactions different from those generated by other types of Web 2.0 communication technologies (Maloy et al., 2017). E-mail connects teachers with students, families, colleagues, and administrative personnel as a means of sharing information. The author is an individual; the audience can be an individual or members of a group. The communication flows one way from the author to the recipient(s) who may respond in an exchange of communications. In texting, information moves from individual author to individual recipient(s), back and forth in digital conversations through writing; texts are not intended as a public forum for others to view and comment.

Teacher blogs and teacher-made classroom websites generate online communications that go from an individual author—the teacher—to a group of readers or followers, usually students, families, or educational colleagues. Teachers use blogs to post information about academic assignments and deadlines, share notes from lectures and PowerPoint presentations, give students resources for learning, and showcase work and reflections done as part of class activities.

Teacher-made classroom websites serve essentially the same functions as teacher blogs, although websites tend to be updated less often. The audience mainly reads but does not respond to the posted material. When audience members do respond, a public discussion may ensue, as with blogs about educational issues where bloggers and audience members offer their views on the latest developments in the field.

Discussion boards and professional learning networks involve multiple authors interacting with multiple audience members. In theory, there is an exchange of ideas and information about topics, with one person serving as the moderator of the site. A post is generated and audience members respond either directly to the post, creating a discussion thread, or by generating a different area for discussion that becomes a new thread.

In contrast to e-mail, texts, blogs, websites, discussion boards, and professional learning networks, wikis create opportunities for multiple authors to communicate with multiple audience members in creative and expressive ways. Ideas and information can be shared quickly using a technology that tech-savvy students tend to embrace as a communication tool. Wikis eliminate the distinction between information generators and information receivers, allowing teachers and students to be in both roles within the same communication system. Wikis evolve over time, growing and expanding as people contribute to pages by adding new material and revising or deleting outdated information. And as two English professors noted, wikis create a shared space where "all readers write the same document"; they move users "toward greater understanding through dialogue" (Cummings & Barton, 2008).

When Ward Cunningham was asked what he thought were the best applications of wikis—what makes wikis "shine" as a technology—he replied, "A wiki works best where you're trying to answer a question that you can't easily pose, where there's not a natural structure that's known in advance to what you need to know" (Venners, 2003). Applying Cunningham's idea to schools, wikis support project-based learning about curriculum topics where students are creating information for wiki pages beyond simply repeating what others have said about that topic. In a wiki format, students can display what they know about topics and their ability to use that knowledge in novel and creative ways.

Cunningham believed in democratic and participatory nature of wikis. This means students and teachers together participate in creating content, express their ideas in their own ways, and contribute as members of a class community in making decisions about what is posted and shared online. "A wiki is timeless," declared Cunningham, "it's a work, it's a product. It's not just the community, it's the product of a community and that community . . . molds it. But when the community leaves the product is still there" (To the Best of Our Knowledge, 2011).

WIKIS IN SCHOOLS

Wikis provide ongoing opportunities for students and teachers to be writers, readers, researchers, designers, analysts, and artists of web-based information displays. In "A Collaboration of Sites and Sounds," an online lesson plan published by the National Council of Teachers of English, students research protest song lyrics about racism, sexism, poverty, war, and other social problems and post their findings on a class wiki—including photos, graphics, and links to add their personal perspectives to their research. The class then listens to and discusses the songs, creating opportunities for students to add more information and resources to each other's wiki pages (Kawakita, 2017).

Yet, despite their potentials for collaborative learning, wikis have not emerged as a widely used K–12 instructional technology. Analyzing a sample drawn from 180,000 publicly available wikis hosted by the company PBworks, a group of Harvard University researchers sought to describe how wikis are actually being used and whether this technology was able to successfully promote twenty-first-century skill development among students in schools in low-income versus more affluent communities (Reich, Murnane, & Willett, 2012).

Summarizing the data, the researchers found just over half of all educational wikis (52 percent) were in grades 9–12, with the rest almost evenly distributed between the middle (28 percent in grades 6–8) and elementary schools (25 percent in grades K–5), while some wikis supported teaching and learning in multiple grades. Wikis were used in each of the primary subject fields of English/language arts (34 percent), social studies (13 percent), science (18 percent), math (13 percent), and computer science (14 percent) along with a variety of other subjects (26 percent) (Reich, Murnane, & Willett, 2012, p. 10).

The Harvard researchers identified four basic types of wikis:

(1) Trial Wikis and Teacher Resource Sharing Sites (40 percent). The largest category, these sites were teacher-created spaces without student interaction or participation that tended not to remain in regular use very long. Most of these sites were static postings of material; what the researchers characterized as "trial balloons that failed to take off" (Reich, Murnane, & Willett, 2012, p. 12). A few sites involved teachers sharing links and resources with other teachers, but these wikis also did not undergo modification or development over time.

(2) Teacher-Content Delivery Sites (34 percent). The second-largest category was teacher-created wikis "with students as receivers of information, not content providers" (Reich, Murnane, & Willett, 2012, p. 12). Teacher-Content Delivery sites provided mainly class-related administrative information: syllabi, homework assignments and due dates, teacher contact information, classroom rules, and school policies. Some sites were created and not updated; others posted new information regularly to keep students informed about the class calendar. Like educational blogs and websites, the teacher was the primary or sole author of the online material.

(3) Individual Student Assignment and Portfolio Sites (25 percent). The third category featured sites where students posted their academic and school-related work online. These wikis ranged from basic sites where students posted their responses to teacher assignments to more complex "multimedia-infused presentations or portfolios on academic topics requiring information organization and crediting of sources." Sites in this category "rarely involved interaction among students" (Reich, Murnane, & Willett, 2012, p. 12).

(4) Collaborative Student Presentation and Workspaces (1 percent). Only a small number of sites featured students and teachers working together to "take full advantage of the collaborative and technological affordances of

wikis" (Reich, Murnane, & Willett, 2012, p. 12). In these sites, students produce multimedia presentations and develop twenty-first-century skills of information consumption and analysis, media literacy, and the online communication of ideas to multiple audiences. Wikis in this category, like many of the sites in the third category, "show promise as learning environments that can prepare students for publishing and collaborative problem solving in a networked age" (Reich, Murnane, & Willett, 2012, p. 13).

Looking at the overall findings, the researchers concluded that while some wikis did generate "an extraordinary diversity of learning activities" that supported "instruction across the curriculum" at all grade levels, most sites started with a promise of regular usage and then faded into nonuse. Only one in four wikis lasted more than 151 days, suggesting that wikis were used for short-term projects only or, in some cases, simply abandoned by their creators shortly after being established online. Even more troubling was that wikis in schools serving low-income students tended to fade away earlier than wikis in other schools. For those low-income students, the lack of opportunities to use wikis constituted another example of the digital divide that separates lower income from more affluent students, schools, and families.

BUILDING WIKIS COLLABORATIVELY

It is the premise of this book that wikis—collaboratively developed and used by students and teachers—can transform teaching and learning in history and humanities classrooms in three distinct ways.

First, students and teachers can access materials and resources on existing educational wikis, including *resourcesforhistoryteachers* and *Teaching Resources for English*, two sites showcased as models in the book.

Second, teachers can construct their own school or classroom wikis, regularly posting material for students to assess and access for teaching and learning activities.

Third, students and teachers as learning partners can collaboratively design, create, and sustain classroom or school wikis.

It is this third use of wikis that may offer the greatest potential for engaging students and sustaining learning. When students and teachers partner in wiki building, they are utilizing digital technology in the ways forecast nearly three decades ago by computer visionary Seymour Papert. At the time, Papert (1980, p. 3) noted how young students are drawn to digital environments that are "fast-paced, immensely compelling and rewarding." By contrast, those same students regarded traditional teaching as "slow, boring, and frankly out of touch" (Papert, 1993, p. 5). Computers, Papert reasoned, are capable of creating mega-change in education because they can generate new collaborative learning environments where students exercise choice and self-determination over what they are learning in and outside of school.

The concept of the child as builder was at the core of Papert's philosophy. Children learn not by doing exercises in books, completing worksheets, or taking multiple-choice tests, but by performing important-to-the-learner, technology-based activities in real-world settings where one's actions have meaningful consequences. In a series of classic experiments, Papert asked children to program commands from the LOGO computer language to direct a turtle-shaped electronic object around a computer screen. As they did, the children were "learning how to exercise control over an exceptionally rich and sophisticated 'micro-world'" (Papert, 1980, p. 12).

Students working with teachers to research, create, and publish wikis can participate in a modern-day application of Papert's vision for promoting deep and lasting learning using technology. Wikis can put students at the center of the learning process. They can allow students to be critical evaluators of online information and creative designers of educational websites. They can propel engagement with academic content from the history and humanities curriculum. The key in wiki use, as it is the key in all uses of technology for learning in schools, is how students and teachers go about answering Papert's (1996, p. 56) famous question, "Will the child program the computer or will the computer program the child?"

AN EXAMPLE OF AN INTERACTIVE WIKI PAGE

The Transcontinental Railroad, that epic nineteenth-century undertaking of technology and engineering, is an often-taught topic in upper elementary, middle, or high schools. The railroad's story encompasses not only the rise of Glided Age corporations and wealth-making entrepreneurs but also, as historian David Hayward Bain (2000, p. xi) reminds us, it includes the experiences of "Native Americans, women of the plains and high country immigrants and other people below the radar scope of traditional historians' 'great men' narratives."

Before computer and the Internet revolution, students and teachers learned about the Transcontinental Railroad (and other history and humanities curriculum topics) using textbooks, primary documents, and other paper materials. In today's classrooms, resources for learning exist as e-texts that can be read, heard, or viewed with tablets, laptops, desktops, smartphones, or other Internet-connected technologies. Students and teachers not only read material on screens, but they can also expand the size of the print, highlight key terms, get dictionary definitions of words, search dynamically within a document, hear words and sentences read aloud, watch embedded videos, assess live links, and complete online writing and review activities.

Today's technologies enable students and teachers to build interactive wiki pages featuring multimodal learning resources as shown by a page on *resourcesforhistoryteachers* wiki for the Transcontinental Railroad.

Page Example: The Transcontinental Railroad

Visit *The Transcontinental Railroad* page: https://resourcesforhis toryteachers.wikispaces.com/Transcontinental+Railroad

The page consists of resources, gathered from multiple free and easily accessible online sources that provide wide-ranging perspectives on the Transcontinental Railroad as an historical event, including:

- An online summary posted on "Digital History," a website from the University of Houston with live links to documents, timelines, historical biographies, images, music, and movie trailers about the Glided Age era.
- An overview of the Glided Age at the website, "U.S. History: Pre-Columbian to the New Millennium" from the Independent Hall Association with live links to the Central Pacific Photographic Museum, a Library of Congress site on maps and railroads, and an online biography of Union Pacific Railroad president Leland Stanford.
- Numerous primary sources, film and video resources, and hidden history/ untold story resources about the experiences of Chinese railway workers, Native Americans, African Americans, and others involved in building the railroad.

Wiki pages such as *The Transcontinental Railroad* with live links to web-based information expand teaching and learning opportunities in history and humanities classrooms, allowing students and teachers to make choices about their educational experience as never before. From wiki pages, they can access videos, podcasts, serious learning games, interactive websites, and other multimodal resources along with written text materials. They can explore material from one source, visit additional linked resources, and return easily to their original document. They can decide which resources to explore and for how long. Education becomes untethered from paper texts and teacher lectures as learners follow their curiosity and interests while engaging in inquiry and analysis.

WIKIS IN DIGITAL-AGE CLASSROOMS

Here are five reasons for integrating wiki technology for learning into digital-age classrooms. First, given the ongoing, wide-ranging print-to-digital transition underway in schools, wikis offer powerful online and computer-based learning experiences for both adults and students. Teachers use wikis to develop curriculum and plan instruction and to manage classroom activities and assignments. Students use wikis to access from anywhere the online learning resources posted by teachers and become directly involved in posting learning materials for others as wiki page makers and builders. Wiki building experiences can happen in conjunction with paper-based materials, blending print and pixel in ways that complement the needs and interests of teachers and students.

Second, since students want to experience connections between their out-of-school and in-school usage of technology, wikis offer the kinds of open-ended, student-initiated learning that mirrors how youngsters use social media platforms and formats. Wikis function as flexible, free-flowing systems, allowing students to express ideas creatively while learning academic content.

Third, since the way technology is integrated determines its impact on students and learning, wikis offer partnerships for teachers and students in activity- and project-based activities. Rather than replacing teachers as central to classroom instruction, wiki technology blends face-to-face student-teacher interactions with inquiry-based learning at multiple grade levels.

Fourth, wikis place students and teachers in vitally important interrelated roles as authors, readers, and evaluators of digital content. Any wiki, in order to grow and evolve, must have multiple authors who contribute continuing new ideas and information to the site. Those ongoing changes give readers reasons to return to the site again and again to see what is new and to learn from it. Students and teachers can be both authors and readers of educational wikis. Being both is especially important for students to gain a sense of ownership of a site to which they are contributing. Teachers benefit too as they involve students in deeper learning of the academic material.

Fifth, successful examples of collaborative wiki building exist and these efforts offer guidance of how to construct wikis. Wikipedia, the world's largest wiki, is evolving in new directions as groups seek to widen its base of contributors and expand the diversity of its content. The Wiki Education Foundation reports that 14,000 college students created or edited 35,000 articles in the past three years (Dewey, 2016). The international Ada Lovelace Day celebration of women's achievements in science, technology, engineering, and math has been the impetus for adding women-centered material to the site. Wikipedia itself has a page on how to conduct an "edit-a-thon" where groups collaboratively update and improve pages. These examples offer just a glimpse of what students and teachers can do as learning partners and wiki builders.

These five points encompass a far-reaching vision for wikis in technology-based learning classroom communities where students and teachers learn the skills of web research and develop the dispositions of digital literacy while gaining academic content knowledge from the history/social studies and humanities curriculum. The chapters ahead offer concrete, practical, readily achievable steps for realizing that vision.

Chapter 2

The Making of a History Wiki

The *resourcesforhistoryteachers* wiki began in 2007 as an online resource for college students at the University of Massachusetts Amherst preparing to take the Massachusetts History or Political Science Teacher Test, exams every prospective educator must pass to receive a license to teach in the state's public schools.

The Massachusetts history and political science teacher tests were, and still are, wide-ranging assessments consisting of one hundred multiple-choice questions and two open-ended essays that encompass historical topics from prehistory to the present day. Test takers must answer questions from U.S. history, world history, geography, political science (in an American and global context) and economics—a scope that takes many college students far beyond their academic knowledge base or comfort levels. "*There are whole continents I never took a course on*," one senior history major stated in amazement after struggling to pass the exam.

Facing the need to ensure that students could succeed on the exam (the state Department of Education had started to publicize the pass rates of test takers at the colleges in the state), Robert Maloy created a three-credit course in the College of Education, "Education 613: New Developments in History and Political Science Education," to review the academic learning standards in the Massachusetts History & Social Science Curriculum Framework, the document on which the test was based.

The course was organized as a weekly study group where students could review the curriculum framework standard-by-standard beginning with ancient civilizations and moving chronologically through world history and U.S. history before finishing with an overview of key material from the standards on government, geography, and economics. Each week students prepared a written study guide for two of the standards and, using a cooperative learning model, shared what they had learned with each other.

Two course design problems were inherent. First, the state's teacher test could include questions based on academic content from nearly 400 separate learning standards, making it very difficult to review of all of them in a single semester. Second, even after discussing the standards in the weekly class, students wanted copies of the notes each of them wrote weekly to prepare for the exam. So Robert made copies of the weekly study guides for each class member to create a notebook of review material. The accumulation of paper proved hard to manage, with missing pages and a costly copying budget. Plus, students found there was no way to readily search their handwritten notes and typed paper study guides to see interconnections between topics, people, and events.

As a solution, one student proposed putting the weekly study guides on a wiki that could be easily accessed, searched, and edited. Launched during the spring 2007 semester, *resourcesforhistoryteachers* began its more than decade-long evolution from a site used by twenty students in one college course annually to a space accessed today by more than a thousand teachers and students worldwide every school day. As the site expanded, the structure of its pages shifted and innovative instructional applications emerged. In this chapter, we discuss the evolution of this wiki into a multifaceted, multimodal resource for history and humanities learning.

A STANDARDS WIKI

Words filled the initial pages of *resourcesforhistoryteachers*—words from the Massachusetts History & Social Science curriculum framework and words from the wiki's first contributors (Maloy et al., 2010). The state's framework consisted of 420 separate learning standards: grades 1 and 2 (People and Places); grade 3 (Massachusetts History); grade 4 (North American Geography/optional standards for ancient China); grade 5 (U.S. History to the Civil War); grade 6 (World Geography); grade 7 (Ancient Civilizations); World History; U.S. History; American Government; and Economics.

To begin the wiki, we made a separate page for each standard and began adding historical content. All of us—course instructors and college students alike—thought of using words to convey ideas and information. Responding to standards such as "Explain the reasons for the French and Indian War, how it led to an overhaul of British imperial policy, and the colonial response to these policies" or "Describe the causes of 19th century European imperialism," we imagined pages with paragraph-length descriptions that would provide readers with the material they needed to understand the topic, learn the information, and pass the teacher test.

Those first pages provided mostly fact-based information, in an all-word format. Only occasionally did a page contributor add a map or picture as a visual resource. Since many standards included topics that neither students nor instructors knew well, entries consisted largely of summaries paraphrasing material from history textbooks, Wikipedia, or other sources. Some students, busy with multiple courses and eager to finish their weekly page assignment, simply copied material directly from books or the web—citing the sources while adding more words to a page.

Text-only pages enticed few readers. Even the students in the Education 613 course admitted that they tended to look only at pages they were assigned, in part because they found the material on the other pages not very interesting to read. We received similar responses from teachers and students in local schools when we asked them to preview the first-draft pages. Teachers said they liked the content, especially connected to state curriculum standards, but they felt the reading level was too advanced for many students. Middle and high school students told us they enjoyed having a digital information source but found the mostly static presentation boring, dense, and off-putting. "Where are the pictures?" said one high school student who, like many of her peers, wanted a more engaging and interactive wiki page format.

PROBLEMS WITH TEXT-HEAVY PAGES

Text-exclusive wiki pages had five problems that prevented them from being used effectively as teaching and learning resources in schools. First, summaries written by college students in our course basically duplicated information that was already available online from Wikipedia, Infoplease, Britannica.com, Encyclopedia.com, and other commonly accessed Internet sites. While it was convenient to have material on a page coded to a specific learning standard, it was also apparent that there was little need for another encyclopedia-like reference for history and humanities content.

Second, text-based pages functioned as a static resource—users could read the information, but there were no ways for them to interact with the material. In this way, *resourcesforhistoryteachers* resembled older forms of broadcast media like television and newspapers that essentially provide a one-way distribution of information from information producer to information consumer. Newer forms of digital media offer interactive information sharing experiences for writers and readers. Using the web, people can send texts and e-mails using mobile phones and other Internet-connected devices; post pictures and videos on social networking sites' submit ratings for and comments about products and services to company websites' or create content to post on blogs, discussion boards, and other media outlets.

Wikis are intended to function as an interactive digital media, offering multiple ways for users to respond to what they are reading or viewing on their pages. As members of a wiki site, students and teachers can edit and revise existing pages or create new ones. They can post comments and offer suggestions for new material. They can organize pages according to their own design, arranging words and images creatively across the screen. Live hyperlinks to other online resources allow students and teachers to explore multiple sources of information at their own speed, dramatically expanding how they can learn about academic topics.

Third, teachers from local schools wanted to use the wiki. No other site, the teachers said, connected historical information and resources to specific learning standards within the state's history and social science curriculum framework. Since teachers were expected to show how their lessons addressed state frameworks, it was useful to them to have material organized by standards. However, while the teachers could envision using the wiki as a curriculum development resource for themselves, they did not see how they could involve students in using the site for in-class teaching and learning activities. Students would not be any more likely to read text-based descriptions of historical topics on a wiki than they were currently reading textbooks or other paper sources of information.

Fourth, text-heavy wiki pages served to perpetuate traditional approaches to the teaching of history, methodologies, and strategies that distance students from learning by placing answers, not questions at the center of the education. Going to those first-draft wiki pages, teachers and students found recitations of facts—the "what happened and when" of historical events—but few opportunities to explore and investigate the how and why of those events. In that initial format, the wiki was essentially replacing pages of a static paper textbook with the pages of a static online website.

Fifth, text-based pages failed to incorporate the amazing new digital technologies and the vast collections of online materials that were becoming available almost yearly. When we began assembling *resourcesforhistoryteachers* in 2006, YouTube had been launched a year earlier, the same year that George W. Bush began releasing his Weekly Presidential Address as a podcast. Apple changed the functions of the smartphone in 2007; iPad appeared in 2010; Snapchat started in 2011; and 3D printing became widely available commercially starting in 2012. The reach of new technologies and online information has now become so widespread and ubiquitous that many of us hardly remember what it was like before them.

Along with new digital technologies, historical organizations, museums, governmental agencies, major newspapers, national and international media outlets, private foundations and institutes, and numerous other educational institutions began posting materials online that heretofore had been seen only by scholars and researchers. These resources include interactive websites that let users explore topics of interest in highly interactive, nonlinear ways; serious learning games that utilize competition and gameplay to teach academic content; timelines and clickable infographics that enable readers to graphically see how events progressed over time; virtual reality simulations and visualizations that take viewers into historical settings in ways never before possible. All of these resources vastly expand how teaching and learning can happen in schools, and none were part of the original pages of the *resourcesforhistoryteachers* wiki.

In retrospect, it is easy to see how the text-based pages happened. All of us as initial contributors were operating within what has been called history's signature pedagogy. "Fact retention," noted teacher Bruce Lesh (2011, pp. 9, 11), has long been "the goal of history education" in K–12 schools and introductory college history courses. Most history teachers do not question a facts-first approach, structuring classes "to make the content to be memorized relevant, interesting, or fun to learn."

Emphasizing academic content coverage through words on a page, *resourcesforhistoryteachers* lacked multimodal resources for open-ended, inquiry-based investigations of people, places, and events. While the early version of the site linked information to learning standards, students and teachers wanted to be able to connect wiki pages to the expanding universe of digital resources that enable web users to read, listen, view, and interact with academic content. The challenge became how to re-envision the site as a source of inquiry-based questions, a resource for historical investigations, a collection of multiple perspectives about people and events, and a source of interactive engagement with history and humanities learning.

VISUAL IMAGES AND MULTIMEDIA RESOURCES

Adding visual or graphic images to each page was the first step in making *resourcesforhistoryteachers* more multimodal. Many educators believe that because humans process information both auditorily and visually, pairing graphics with words is a powerful and proven instructional strategy (Pomerance, Greenberg, & Walsh, 2015).

Visual images include photographs, pictures, paintings, maps, diagrams, political cartoons, and other images that inform and enliven learning resources. Visuals—left justified, right justified, or centered on a wiki page—serve to highlight key people, document key events, and reveal key themes related to a standard while attracting the interest of readers and viewers. Images can also be formatted from smaller to larger size, depending on their location on a page.

In selecting images, we used public domain and freely licensed materials found online at Wikimedia Commons, a vast database of more than twenty-eight million media files sponsored by the Wikimedia Foundation. Our goal is to create variety among the images on a page. Over time, students and teachers began adding images as well, so now most pages combine words, images, and online links to form a multimodal reading, viewing, and learning experience.

Historical photographs are an especially compelling resource in the ways they promote learning and understanding for many page readers. A standard on important battles of World War II might include a photo of Russian soldiers at the Battle of Stalingrad, Allied troops landing at Normandy, U.S. Marines hoisting the flag at Iwo Jima, or a European city street destroyed by aerial bombardment. Each image conveys the destruction and horror of modern warfare.

Standards that focus on long-ago events need a wider variety of images to convey meaning. For the Bill of Rights, there are no photographs of James Madison drafting the amendments or Federalists and Anti-Federalists debating the powers of the new government. To present the drafting of the nation's constitution, we selected a photo of a 1996 five-cent postage stamp commemorating the 175th anniversary of the event; a 1900 Ernest Normand drawing of King John signing the Magna Carta; a 1993 James Madison commemorative coin; a 1766 Benjamin Blythe portrait of Abigail Adams; and a painting of the First Federal Congress from the Architect of the U.S. Capitol.

Every historical concept or event is an opportunity to blend visual materials to engage readers and promote understanding. Table 2.1 lists the pictorial

Table 2.1. Pictorial Images Included on Two Wiki Pages

World history II.11: Describe the causes of nineteenth-century European imperialism	*U.S. history I.41: Explain the policies and consequences of Reconstruction*
Map: Territorial Claims of the British Empire, 1919	**Illustration**: Freedmen Voting in New Orleans, 1867 from *Harper's Weekly*
Painting: *Lord Clive Meeting with Mir Jafar after the Battle of Plassey*, 1757 by Francis Hayman (1760)	**Photograph**: Robert Smalls, an African American politician who served in Congress between 1868 and 1889
1897 Textbook Illustration: Berlin Conference, 1885	**Illustration**: Senate as a Court of Impeachment of Andrew Johnson, 1868 from *Harper's Weekly*
Photograph: Belgian King Leopold II	**Map**: Order of States Ratifying the 13th Amendment
Photograph: Journalist E. D. Morel who sought to expose abuses of Belgian colonialism in the Congo	**Illustration**: Account of the 1866 Memphis Riot from *Harper's Weekly*
1913 Map: Religions in Africa as a guide for missionaries seeking to convert Africans to Christianity	**Photograph**: Justice John Marshall Harlan, sole dissenter in *Plessy v. Ferguson* (1896)

images selected for a world history standard on the causes of nineteenth-century European imperialism and a U.S. history standard on the polices and consequences of Reconstruction after the Civil War. The images were placed throughout the page, from top to bottom to give readers visual connections to people, events, and ideas found within the standard.

Page Examples: 19th Century European Imperialism and Reconstruction after the Civil War

Visit the *19th-Century European Imperialism* page: https://resources forhistoryteachers.wikispaces.com/WHII.11
Visit the *Reconstruction after the Civil War* page:
https://resourcesforhistoryteachers.wikispaces.com/US1.41

Adding photographs and images to wiki pages emphasizes two instructional functions. First, online pages become more visually interesting for students, especially younger readers, many of whom respond favorably to viewing pictures instead of printed text on a page. "Every picture tells a story," noted two social studies educators who found that historical images "help students connect with history on a personal level while learning and practicing essential skills in critical thinking, analysis, synthesis, research and empathy" (McCormick & Hubbard, 2011).

Second, creatively chosen images are compelling images for teachers to show and discuss with students in class. Photographs, maps, paintings that represent historical events, charts and graphs, political cartoons, and other images help students to connect and recall standards, people, and events that can form the basis for deeper academic inquires and investigations.

Multimedia Resources

To further change the form and function of the wiki, we expanded our definition of the term "resources" from the title *resourcesforhistoryteachers*. Resources are materials that support accomplishing one's goals easily, quickly, and successfully, and they are either paper or digital. Online digital resources include not only text-based websites but many types of multimedia materials that prepare classroom teachers to develop student-centered, standards-based curriculum lessons, engage students in inquiry-based history and humanities learning, and prepare test takers for a test.

Multimedia resources support learning for almost every student; as learning theorist Richard E. Mayer noted, "People learn better from words and pictures than from words alone" (2009, pp. 1, 3, 5). Drawing on research into how students experience words and visuals in educational settings, Mayer saw multimedia learning having three dimensions: "delivery media"—computer screens, teachers at microphones, images displayed on whiteboards; "presentation mode"—how words and pictures are combined in a learning situation, and "sensory modalities"—how students listen, view, and/or interact with material (2009, p. 3). Mayer sees effective teaching and learning happening when material appears in "verbal" and "pictorial" forms (2009, p. 5).

Page Example: Charles Darwin and the Theory of Evolution

Visit the *Charles Darwin and the Theory of Evolution* page here: http://resourcesforhistoryteachers.wikispaces.com/Charles+Darwin+and+the+Theory+of+Evolution

A class studying Charles Darwin and the discoveries that led to his theories of natural selection and evolution as part of a combined science and social studies unit might read text-based accounts from a textbook or website. These activities provide students with one type of educational experience while multimedia materials expand the learning. On a page devoted to Darwin, students can view an online animation of Darwin's life featuring audio, music, and pictures from the National Center for Scientific Research; consult an interactive map of Darwin's voyages from the BBC; see pictures of the Galapagos Islands, now a United Nations World Heritage site; or watch a YouTube video reenactment of a famous Oxford debate between Thomas Huxley (defending Darwin) and Bishop Samuel Wilberforce (defending biblical accounts of creation); and play *Who Wants to Live a Million Years?*—an online game about natural selection and survival of species.

TYPES OF INTERACTIVE RESOURCES

Designing wiki pages interactively and multimodally, we included six categories of teaching and learning items commonly used in history/social studies/humanities classes:

1. primary sources;
2. maps, interactive geography resources, and timelines;
3. film and video resources;
4. simulations, visualizations, and serious learning games;
5. lesson plans and teaching resources;
6. multicultural, women's, and LGBTQ history materials.

The goal was for every page to have links to resources from all or most of these six categories. To highlight the type and location of these materials on the pages, we chose icons to represent each resource. Icons provide readers with a quick recognizable pictorial indicator of what resources are linked in a section of a page.

Primary Sources

Primary sources, indicated by an old-time manuscript icon, include documents, artifacts, journals, diaries, newspapers, literature, artwork, speeches, and other first-hand accounts of events that allow "students to explore the thoughts, values and biases of the people that they find walking through history." As evidence of the historical record, sources can be defined broadly, "all the remains of a time period, everything that people created and were then, somehow, by intent or by chance in some way preserved until today" (Clabough et al., 2016, p. 3).

Core information for history and humanities learning, primary sources "remove the distance that students feel from historical events;" they "connect them more intimately to the past" (Symcox, 1991, p. 4). Reading and viewing primary sources invite a "sense of 'being there'," where students can see "history through the eyes of the very people who were making historical decisions." Primary materials can help students to realize that history is people made. Each of us—children, adolescents, and adults—are history-making individuals whose choices and decisions make history a day-by-day, event-by-event story that is constantly being created and remembered.

Primary sources contribute to how students and teachers explore learning standards. A standard on the accomplishments of ancient Greek civilization might include links to the *Iliad* and the *Odyssey* as well as plays by Sophocles, Euripides, and Aristophanes. Studying the Civil War and the presidency of Abraham Lincoln, they can read the text of Gettysburg Address, the House Divided Speech, the Second Inaugural Address, and the Emancipation Proclamation as well as writing by Olaudah Equiano, Harriet Jacobs, Sojourner Truth, Frederick Douglass, and other less well-known abolitionists.

To advance student learning, primary sources should include visual as well as text-based materials, for, as two history educators noted, "the modern world demands that students be able to navigate a reality dominated by visual information" (Austin & Thompson, 2014, p. 9). Examining visual primary sources is a way for students to "develop the ability to look at an image, analyze it, decode it" as they gain the capacity to "read images in the same way that they read text" (Austin & Thompson, 2014, p. 9).

Extensive collections of primary source materials exist online from the Library of Congress, including *American Memory* featuring written and spoken words, sound recordings, still and moving images, prints, maps, and sheet music documenting the nation's national experience. *America's*

Story from America's Library has multimedia materials for elementary and middle grade students. The *National Jukebox* has an extensive collection of historical sound recordings. The teacher section of *Teaching with Primary Sources* includes free student discovery e-books for primary source exploration accompanied by document sets and lesson plans. The *African American Mosaic* has materials for the study of black history and culture.

Other primary source collections on the web include archives that no single textbook could hold. "DocTeach" from the National Archives, the "Internet History Sourcebook Project" coordinated by Paul Halsall at Fordham University, "America in Class," primary source materials linked to the Common Core State Standards from the National Humanities Center, "A Brush with History: Paintings from the National Portrait Gallery," and "The Vault," a repository of declassified FBI records are free online resources that bring historical materials to the arts and humanities curriculum.

Maps and Interactive Geography Materials

Maps, both static and interactive, bring a vital visual dimension to history/social studies learning. They help students and teachers locate countries and regions as part of geographic study; they show the movement of people during periods of migration and movement; they offer visualizations of trends and patterns from the rise and fall of empires to the flow of goods and trade throughout the world. These are represented by an ancient map icon on *resourcesforhistoryteachers*.

There are extensive geography resources freely available online. "The World Factbook" from the Central Intelligence Agency (CIA) has information about all the countries of the world. "WorldMapper" from the University of Sheffield resizes land areas according to categories of wealth, poverty, and education for different historical time periods. "Population Pyramids of the World from 1950 to 2010" has interactive graphs showing trends for different countries and regions. "The Mapping History Project" from the University of Oregon provides animated representations of historical events in American, European, Latin American, and African history.

Timelines

Timelines, denoted by a green timeline icon, support and encourage chronological thinking, a skill "at the heart of historical reasoning" (National Center for History in the Schools, 1996). Knowing the sequence of events enables students and teachers to explore relationships among people and events while establishing a framework for understanding historical causality. History taught as disconnected facts means "students don't develop a sense of historic era and they don't connect individual events to larger movements and themes" (Fillpot, n.d.).

Visually engrossing timelines online include the *Heilbrunn Timeline of Art History* from Metropolitan Museum of Art and *eHistory* from The Ohio State University. Students can also create their own timelines, in 2D or 3D, with paper, text, and pictures or using digital tools and computer apps, as in the following lesson on the Scientific Revolution (Jelen, 2011). In pairs or small groups, students build timelines of the accomplishments of men and women scientists, from Galileo and Newton to Margaret Cavendish and Maria Sibylla Merian. Students then view and comment about what they have learned from each other's work. The collective efforts of the students create an overall timeline that can be posted on a class website, blog, or wiki. Student work can also be used to construct wiki pages for scientists such as this page for Mary Anning.

Page Example: Mary Anning: Fossil Hunter and Paleontologist

Visit *Mary Anning: Fossil Hunter and Paleontologist* page here:
http://resourcesforhistoryteachers.wikispaces.com/Mary+Anning%2C +Fossil+Finder+and+Paleontologist

Films and Videos

Film and video resources, identified by an old-style reel-to-reel movie camera icon, include moving images from historical documentaries and newsreel footage to commercially made movies and television shows to visual materials posted on YouTube and other video-sharing websites. PowerPoint and Prezi slideshows are included in this category as a widely used way to widen history learning multimodally.

Film and video can be effective learning resources in history and humanities classrooms for three reasons. First, some film and video can be viewed as primary sources that offer insights into different cultural and social contexts. Second, these materials open opportunities for thoughtful debates about the meaning and interpretation of events. Third, "they engage today's visually attuned students in a direct, visceral manner that written documents may have difficulty achieving" (Fuller, 1999).

Viewing YouTube is a staple of history and humanities instruction at most grade levels. Students and teachers watch documentaries, news shows, historical reenactments, scenes from movies and television shows, interviews with historical figures, important speeches, and many other types of moving images. YouTube is not the sole source of video resources. There are compelling materials available from Ted Talks, iTunes U, Kahn Academy, Internet Archive, historical organizations, museums, college and university departments, government agencies, and independent presenters.

Video materials can visually expand how students and teachers think about time, people, and events. For example, a wiki page on the relationship of English settlers to the indigenous people in North America might include video materials about the 1704 Raid on Deerfield (Massachusetts), the Pequot War and King Philip's War as well as other native/settler encounters. A standard on the major contributions of Roman civilization could feature a video explaining the Twelve Tables as a cornerstone of the Roman legal system, and to illustrate Roman engineering, a video on the construction of Roman baths.

Simulations, Visualizations, and Serious Learning Games

Simulations, visualizations, and serious learning games have three essential components: (1) they engage learners and require "them to actively participate in comprehending the content"; (2) they utilize multiple modalities in delivering information, including video, audio, kinesthetic; and (3) they include assessment components "that test and inform learners about their understanding of the material" (Shank, 2014, p. xii). A tablet computer screen icon marks their location on each wiki page.

A "visualization is any graphic that organizes meaningful information in a multidimensional spatial form," and include interactive maps, diagrams, infographics, and virtual reality presentations (Staley, 2013, p. xi). While printed text is one-dimensional, visualizations deliver information in two- and three-dimensional forms. As such, visualizations can challenge historians, teachers, and students who are "word people," more familiar with studying primary sources, reading textbooks, and writing essays. But, argues David Staley, "using computers strictly to store, transmit, and retrieve words is akin to using an automobile only to park" (2013, p. xii). As a component of multiple ways of learning and a compliment to text-based readings, visualizations offer expansive ways to organize, present, and remember history/social studies information.

A web-based simulation is a "computer game that dynamically represents one or more real-world processes or systems in the past" (McCall, 2011). Such games "immerse students in a world of conflicting goals and choices where they have the power to make decisions and experience (virtually) the consequences of those decisions."

Serious learning games use the interactive, entertainment, and play dimensions of video games to deliver academic content to students. The intent is to learn while having fun. All games have four defining traits, "a goal, rules, a feedback system and voluntary participation." Other dimensions commonly associated with games—"interactivity, graphics, narrative, rewards, competition, virtual environments, or the idea of winning"—serve to "reinforce and enhance these four core elements" (McGonigal, 2011).

Visualizations, simulations, and serious games build on James Paul Gee's (2007) pioneering premise that the theory of learning built into effective video games features the essential principles that students and teachers need to organize successful academic learning in school classrooms—students asking meaningful questions, evaluating and analyzing sources, drawing distinctions between important and less important information, analyzing interrelationships among people and systems, and deriving interpretations based on evidence and experience.

Multicultural, Women's, and LGBTQ History Materials

Multicultural, women's, and LGBTQ history resources are online materials whose perspectives challenge and expand the views of students and students about people and society. A green globe marks African American history materials, a female rose identifies women's history materials, a sand painting signifies Native American resources, a map of Central and South America is used for Latino history, and a rainbow flag signifies LGBTQ (Lesbian, Gay, Bisexual, Transgender, Queer) resources.

Most curriculum frameworks and mainstream textbooks, however, organize historical study around what historian Ronald Takaki (2008, pp. 4, 5, 6) has called "the Master Narrative of American History" that holds "our country was settled by European immigrants, and Americans are White." Since "our education system as a whole has not integrated the histories of *all* people," Takaki urges race and ethnicity be studied "inclusively and comparatively" using narratives and stories from multiple sources because "a more inclusive curriculum is also a more accurate one."

To build a broader, more inclusive curriculum, Howard Zinn (2015, p. 10) proposes history be taught by revealing, not concealing "fierce conflicts of interest (sometimes exploding, most often repressed) between conquerors and conquered, masters and slaves, capitalists and workers, dominators and dominated in race and sex." Following Zinn, we have made it a goal to add diverse history resources to every wiki page that highlight the experiences of different peoples, genders, ethnicities, and cultures.

We have also continued adding categories to the pages, each with its own icon: a quill in an ink holder for historical biographies; a dollar sign for economics resources; an image of the scales of justice for resources dealing with courts and the law; a picture of a book for works of important fiction and nonfiction literature; and a picture of the White House for material about American presidents.

ASSEMBLING MULTIMODAL WIKI PAGES

The Coming of the American Revolution wiki page uses the six categories of interactive resources to assemble a collection of multimodal resources on a standards-based wiki. The page is based on a Massachusetts curriculum framework standard: *Analyze how Americans resisted British policies before 1775 and analyze the reasons for the American victory and the British defeat during the Revolutionary War* (Massachusetts Department of Education, 2003, p. 65).

Page Example: The Coming of the American Revolution

Visit *The Coming of the American Revolution* page:
https://resourcesforhistoryteachers.wikispaces.com/USI.4

Two focus questions frame the page: "How did Americans resist British policies before 1775?" and "What were the reasons for the American victory and the British defeat?" In answering the questions, the page is divided into the following sections: Overview; Patriots and Causes of the Revolution; Boston Tea Party and Boston Massacre; African Americans and the Revolution; Women and the Revolution; the "Washington Crossing the Delaware" painting; and the Treaty of Paris.

Pictorial images illustrate the key topics:

- 1760s political cartoon depicting repeal of the Stamp Act
- 1925 postage stamp honoring Nathan Hale
- Painting: "Americans Throwing Cargoes of the Tea Ships into the River, at Boston," W. D. Cooper *The History of North America*, 1789
- Painting: "Washington Leading Continental Army to Valley Forge," William B. T. Trego 1883
- Painting: "Colonial Soldiers at the Siege of Yorktown," Jean-Baptiste-Antoine DeVerger, 1781 (the African American soldier is supposedly from the first Rhode Island Regiment)
- 1859 print of "Molly Pitcher at the Battle of Monmouth"
- Painting: "Washington Crossing the Delaware," Emmanuel Luetze 1851.

Primary source materials include a link to the text of David Ramsey's *The History of the American Revolution*—the first American national history written by an American revolutionary and printed in America.

There are links to "The Able Doctor, or America Swallowing the Bitter Drought" (1774), a political cartoon supporting Great Britain's right to tax the colonies; "Lord Dunmore's Proclamation" (1775) that offered freedom to slaves that fought for the British, and the "Treaty of Paris" (1783) that ended the war. In addition, there are materials posted by Annenberg Learner, the Library of Congress, Colonial Williamsburg, PBS, the National Council of Teachers of English (NCTE), and the Gilder Lehrman Institute of American History.

The page has links exploring the roles of African Americans and women during the Revolution. This includes hidden history and untold information about the First Rhode Island Regiment, a unit in the Continental Army that included several companies of black soldiers. Overall, some 5,000 African Americans served in the Continental Army and several hundred more served at sea.

Women's history links include material on Molly Pitcher and the Battle of Monmouth as well as whether she was an actual person or a composite figure drawn from multiple accounts. There are also links to brief biographies for other notable women, including Abigail Adams, Esther Reed, Phillis Wheatley, Sybil Ludington, Mercy Otis Warren, Betsy Ross, and Martha Washington. The page also has lesson plans for analyzing Emanuel Leutze's painting of Washington Crossing the Delaware and for understanding the lives of everyday soldiers in the Continental Army.

Like *The Coming of the American Revolution*, all pages in *resourcesforhistoryteachers* and its sister wiki, *Teaching Resources for English*, feature visual images, links to primary and secondary source materials, and multimedia and multicultural resources, as in the following examples from pages for topics in world history, geography, government, economics, and poetry writing.

Page Examples: The Cold War, Antarctica, Roles of Citizens, Function of Profit in a Market Economy, Poetry Writing

World History: Visit the *Cold War* page:
https://resourcesforhistoryteachers.wikispaces.com/WHII.30
Geography: Visit the *Antarctica* page:
https://resourcesforhistoryteachers.wikispaces.com/Antarctica
Visit the *Roles of Citizens* including Voting page:
https://resourcesforhistoryteachers.wikispaces.com/USG.5.2
Visit the *Function of Profit in a Market Economy* page:
https://resourcesforhistoryteachers.wikispaces.com/E.2.5

Approaches to *Poetry Writing*
https://teachingresourcesforenglish.wikispaces.com/Approaches+
to+Writing+Poetry

STRATEGIES FOR BUILDING WIKI PAGES WITH STUDENTS

Essential strategies for building wiki pages include the following:

- *Limit links to Wikipedia or other online encyclopedias when writing summaries or overviews of historical events, people and literature.* Look for links to online open content digital resources'; for example, "Digital History" (University of Houston); "America's Story" (Library of Congress); "Key Milestones" (Office of the Historian, U.S. Department of State); "History by Era" (Gilder Lehrman Institute of American History); "World History Matters" (George Mason University); "American Passages: A Literary Survey" (Annenberg Learner); "Poems and Poets" (Poetry Foundation); "Poetry through the Ages" (WebExhibits).
- *Limit the use of primary source materials found on sites or on the pages of overtly political organizations.* As alternatives, there are many exemplary sites for locating primary source materials, including for U.S. history, "American Memory" (Library of Congress); "America in Class" (National Humanities Center); "DocsTeach" (National Archives); and "Many Pasts: U.S. Survey Course on the Web" (George Mason University). Paul Halsall's "Internet History Sourcebook Project" from Fordham University has multiple world history resources including source books on ancient, medieval, global, African, East Asian, Islamic, and Indian history. "Finding World History" from George Mason University is a starting place for locating primary sources in a global context.
- *Incorporate a wide variety of visual images and multimedia resources*, including videos, audio, photographs, artwork, paintings, interactive timelines and other still or moving images. YouTube videos are allowed, after checking the author's identity to determine who is posting the material. As much as possible, we choose to access public domain and creative common licensed images—the site "Wikimedia Commons" is a most valuable resource. "Smarthistory" from Kahn Academy is a source for videos and essays on art history; "Internet Archive" has historic moving images that are in the public domain; "The Object of History" from National Museum of American History is a site for creating virtual exhibits based on artifacts from everyday life and material culture.
- *Guide students to multicultural resources for uncovering hidden histories and untold stories about the past.* Here, teachers can find topics for

students to research rather than asking students to find topics and resources on their own. "Teaching a People's History" from the Zinn Education Project is one source of hidden histories as are the books *A People's History of the United States* and *A Young People's History of the United States* by Howard Zinn, *An Indigenous People's History of the United States* by Roxanne Dunbar-Ortiz, *A People's History of the World* by Chris Harman, and *Lies My Teacher Told Me* by James Loewen. Bill Bigelow has a list of unsung social justice heroes on the Zinn Education Project website. "Women in World History," a website from George Mason University offers women's history resources; "OutHistory" has resources learning about LGBTQ history.

- *Use online biographies from academic and historical organizations.* For-profit historical/author biography sites such as Biography.com, Biography Online or Infoplease may have useful summaries of people's lives, but they feature numerous product advertisements as well as links to unrelated information and sites. Look for biographies posted by libraries, museums, historical organizations, foundations, universities, or government agencies. Obituaries from major newspapers are another source of information about the lives and times of notable persons.

  The *Writer's Almanac with Garrison Keillor* offers summaries of the life and times of historical figures on their birthdays. The *Google Doodles Archive* has links to more than 2,000 visuals, short videos, and text summaries about notable people and events. The *Internet Public Library's Biography* section organizes its biographies according to artists and architects; authors; entertainers; musicians and composers; politicians and rulers; and scientists and inventors. "Unsung Heroes: Encouraging Students to Appreciate Those Who Fought for Social Justice" from the Zinn Education Project offers a starting point for expansive historical biography projects (Bigelow, 2004).

- *Avoid online study guide sites such as CliffNotes, SparkNotes, or eNotes when searching for book synopses and author/poet biographies.* Instead locate sites from academic organizations that explore a book or the book's author. Book reviews from newspapers like the *New York Times* or "The New York Review of Books" and "C-Span American Writers" are also sources for summarizing a book and its historical relevance. Book summaries from major publishers can also provide engaging introduction to fiction and nonfiction literature.

- *Direct students to reliable sites for engaging lesson plans and teaching resources* such as "NEH EDSITEment Lesson Plans" (National Endowment for the Humanities); "Smithsonian's History Explorer" (National Museum of American History); "National History Education Clearinghouse" (George Mason University); "Labor History Curriculum" (Illinois Labor History Society); and Teaching American History (George Mason University).

Finally, wiki pages are meant to evolve and change—interactively and collaboratively as new contributors build on the efforts of prior users. *resourcesforhistoryteachers* reflects this process as college students and classroom teachers add resources and we as editors make revisions as well.

The evolution and change of wiki pages has produced three major outcomes. First, some pages change often while other pages develop more slowly, reflecting the interest of different contributors. Even when college students in our wiki development course are assigned a page, their contributions vary in length and quality. A highly motivated student may work extensively on a page while another member of the class may add little new material. We have learned that wiki pages evolve differently over time.

Second, we have chosen not to try to strictly standardize the content of pages by requiring that the same resources be located in the same places or in the same top-to-bottom order. Some pages have more primary source materials while others feature more multimedia and multicultural resources. Pages have varying amounts of written text to complement pictorial images and external links. As a result, each page has an evolving style and look, making using the wiki an ongoing process of investigation and discovery for students and teachers alike.

Third, the process of constantly revisiting and revising pages has enabled us to identify strategies for locating (*accessing*) and evaluating (*assessing*) reliable, historically accurate, and student-centered teaching and learning resources—the foundation of information and digital literacy and the topic we explore in the next chapter.

Chapter 3

Developing Digital Literacies

Fake news became big news throughout the 2016 presidential election. Social media was awash with fabricated stories, bogus chain e-mails, and doctored documents purporting, among other claims, that the Pope had endorsed Donald Trump; Hillary Clinton was suffering from serious undisclosed medical problems; the Republican candidate overwhelmingly won the popular vote; and paid protestors were being bused into American cities to dispute the election results. While falsehoods and untruths have long been part of American politics, the web and huge Internet companies have now "made it possible for fake news to be shared nearly instantly with millions of users and have been slow to block it from their sites" (the *New York Times* Editorial Board, 2016).

Just days after the election, Sam Wineburg and colleagues from the Stanford University History Education Group (2016) released findings of a study investigating the civic reasoning skills of 7,000 middle school to college-age students. Across the grade levels, the researchers were "taken back by students' lack of preparation in evaluating the credibility" of what they read and viewed on the web. The study included students from underresourced inner city schools in Los Angeles and well-funded suburban schools outside Minneapolis as well as undergraduates from elite college and large public universities.

Across age groups and irrespective of school settings, students struggled to determine whether a news story or a sponsored post was more reliable (80 percent believed the sponsored content was a legitimate news story). They were unable to decide whether to trust that an unattributed photograph of deformed daises had actually been taken at the site of Japan's Fukushima Daiichi nuclear disaster; 80 percent simply accepted the photo as authentic without checking any resources. In other tasks, students had difficulty searching online to verify claims about a controversial topic, identifying the strengths and weaknesses of an online video, or explaining why a tweet might or might not provide reliable information about a political issue.

Wineburg's investigations are the latest in a series of studies where researchers have found that the majority numbers of elementary and secondary school students assume that all or most of what they read and view online is accurate and true (Coiro et al., 2015; Kahne & Bowyer, 2016; Ofcom, 2015; Purcell et al., 2012). Naïve consumers of web and social media content, students of all ages have great difficulty distinguishing between carefully vetted information and falsely made claims, as Donald Leu and his colleagues from the University of Connecticut found more than a decade ago when they showed middle school students *Save the Pacific Northwest Tree Octopus*, a satirical website that first appeared in 1998 and is still online today.

The Tree Octopus site purports to be the home of a campaign to save an endangered species from extinction. At first examination, its web pages appear genuine—there are colorful graphics, scientific-looking pictures, attention-grabbing headlines, and pages and pages of seemingly academic language. But, the tree octopus is a completely make-believe creature—its biology, ecology, and history presented in amusing language and clever parody. The tree octopus, declares the site, faces threats from "booming populations of its natural predators, including the bald eagle and Sasquatch."

While all of this might seem to be solid satire and laughable, nearly all the youngsters in the study accepted the tree octopus as being real. Even when told the site was a hoax, many of the students—chosen by teachers because they were considered the strongest readers in their classes—still did not believe they had been fooled. The students' responses were not what the researchers expected, as Professor Leu explained in a 2011 interview, "We were quite surprised that none of the students did anything to evaluate the site. That is, they didn't Google it, they didn't try and locate who the author was, try and determine who had created this" (Cherry, 2011). It was as if the students assumed that since the site had lots of text-based information presented in an academic-looking format, "it must be reliable and I can use it in my homework."

In an age of instantly available online information, these findings highlight the importance of students developing skills of Internet comprehension and evaluation—what educators call "digital literacy." This chapter defines digital literacy and discusses how teachers and students can collaborate to become critical evaluators of web and social media information. When students go online, there is no librarian or fact checker immediately available to prescreen what they find for academic use. Instead, teachers and students must learn how to carefully locate (*access*) and critically evaluate (*assess*) online resources for accuracy, reliability, and credibility. Realizing the issues that students encounter when doing web research, there are strategies for selecting academic material for learning with a website evaluation process called select/consider/reject that can be used to build class wikis for history and humanities learning.

DEFINING DIGITAL LITERACY

Digital literacy encompasses modern-day dimensions of computer and information literacy along with the traditional skills of reading, writing, and communicating. According to the American Library Association, digital literacy is "the ability to use information and communication technologies to *find, understand, evaluate, create,* and *communicate* digital information. Basic reading and writing skills are foundational; and true digital literacy requires both cognitive and technical skills" (ALA Digital Literacy Taskforce, 2013).

Digital literacy is part of a broader concept of information literacy, defined by the Association of College & Research Libraries (2000) as being able to "recognize when information is needed and have the ability to locate, evaluate and use effectively the needed information." While information literacy includes information in all its formats—textual, pictorial, mathematical, musical, and artistic expressions—digital literacy refers to information found in online environments.

Multiple educational organizations have affirmed the importance of teaching digital literacy to students. The Common Core State Standards for English Language Arts and Literacy in History/Social Studies (2016) state students need to be able to "determine the central ideas or information of a primary or secondary source" and "integrate and evaluate multiple sources of information presented in diverse formats and media in order to address a question or solve a problem."

The International Society for Technology in Education (ISTE) makes being able to "critically curate a variety of resources using digital tools" the basis of its "Knowledge Constructor" Standard for Students (2016). The Partnership for 21st Century Learning (P21) defines information and communication technology literacy as using "technology as a tool to research, organize, evaluate, and communicate information" (n.d.). The College, Career & Civic Life (C3) Framework for Social Studies State Standards emphasizes students "developing questions and planning inquires, gathering and evaluating sources, and communicating and critiquing conclusions" (National Council for the Social Studies, 2013, p. 12).

What the C3 framework notes—and classroom teachers know all too well—is rapid access to online resources "does not translate automatically to their wise use" (National Council for the Social Studies, 2013, p. 12).

Students' tendencies are to go online and repeat whatever they find there as accurate information.

According to a national sample of Advanced Placement (AP) and National Writing Project (AP/NWP) teachers, 94 percent of students use Google as a digital research tool, followed by Wikipedia (used by 75 percent), and You-Tube (used by 52 percent). Slightly less than half consult their peers or use Cliff Notes to get information for their research. Only 12 percent of students use books (Purcell et al., 2012). Observing these numbers, researchers from the Pew Internet Research Project concluded that in many schools, the definition of research has "shifted from a relatively slow process of intellectual curiosity and discovery to a fast-paced, short-term exercise aimed at locating just enough information to complete an assignment" (Purcell et al., 2012).

In the view of the AP/NWP teachers, search engines offer students access to a wider range of information than ever before, but wide access is not automatically a positive development. Eighty-seven percent of the teachers said Internet search tools distract students from academic work while shortening attention spans; 76 percent said search engines have "conditioned students to expect to be able to find information quickly and easily"; 71 percent believe search tools discourage students from doing deeper investigations or cross-checking their findings using multiple information sources.

Teaching students how to critically evaluate and utilize online information is a vital component of history and humanities education. To understand history and society, teachers and students must examine information, analyze primary and secondary sources, read multiple accounts and perspectives, and develop interpretations and explanations based on the best available evidence. As the University of California Berkeley Library (2012) straightforwardly declared, "The burden is on you—the reader—to establish the validity, authorship, timeliness, and integrity of what you find."

CHALLENGES OF ONLINE INFORMATION

There are three factors that make it difficult for students and teachers to distinguish fraudulent from credible information in online environments. First is the "sheer volume of information" available online. Second, in checking the accuracy of web-based information, users must often rely on the web itself. Third, online information is always changing rapidly (Burbules, 2001).

Nearly two decades ago, educators Nicholas Burbules and Thomas Callister (2000) identified four basic types of "troublesome" online content:

• "Misinformation" (information that is false, out of date, or incomplete in a misleading way);

- "Malinformation" (information that is harmful or damaging);
- "Messed-up information" (information that confusingly presented so it cannot be clearly understood);
- "Mostly useless information" (information that is trivial and inconsequential). Those who are unprepared to recognize and respond to these four challenges are susceptible to online hoaxes, scams, swindles, and manipulations.

In response, Burbules (2001, pp. 445–447) proposed the strategies for judging the credibility of website information that have become standard practice.

- First, look for "markers or 'proxies' of credibility"—including the look and layout of a site ("If it is well-designed and carefully maintained, it is more likely to be from a serious source"). Identify the author, see whether the material comes from an academic or commercial source, and determine if the site is updated on a regular basis.
- Second, crosscheck or verify web-based information with material from more than one other source, both online and print.
- Third, rely on website evaluations done by trustworthy sources, such as academic, not-for-profit, and media organizations.
- Fourth, participate in "communities ('rings') of like-minded people who share a common interest or concern" as a way to exchange reliable information.

University of Rhode Island professor Julie Coiro (2014) proposes that students and teachers focus on four dimensions of online information: Relevance, Accuracy, Bias/Perspective, and Reliability. Relevance and Accuracy relate to a site's informational content, while Bias/Perspective and Reliability focus on who is posting the material and why. As naive users of the web, most students are not prepared to address these four dimensions, tending to equate the look and volume of a site with cred-ibility while failing to identify key information about a site's author(s) and publishing details.

Guidelines from the American Library Association identify six criteria for evaluating web resources: Accuracy, Authority, Objectivity, Currency, Coverage, and Relevancy. Accuracy assesses whether the information on a site is up-to-date and factually correct and whether sources have been correctly cited. Authority refers to the author and/or publisher of a site and whether the author/organization is a scholar or academic or historical orga-nization; a teacher, students or school system; an independent researcher or for-profit organization; or some other individual or group. Objectivity relates to the purpose of a site; whether the goal is to inform or to persuade, sell, or entertain. Relevancy means that the material is related to the topic being studied.

To teach students to critically assess the quality and usefulness of web content, technology educator Kathy Schrock (2015) has proposed the "5 Ws of Website Evaluation." Widely adopted by teachers and schools, the five Ws include:

1. "Who" is a site's author and/or publisher? Has online content been written by knowledgeable researchers and commentators and published by credible organizations, institutions, or companies. Students can see if a site has a link for more information about the author and the publisher.
2. "What" is the purpose of a site? Is the site intended to provide information and resources, sell products and services, advocate for an idea or cause, or engage readers and viewers academically? Examining a site's purpose involves identifying a website's domain (.com, .edu, .gov, .org) and whether a site's designation may impact its usefulness as a teaching and learning resource. Many .com sites are more focused on sales and marketing than academic or historical analysis.
3. "When" was a site created, and when was it last updated? Is the information up-to-date, historically accurate, and academically relevant?
4. "Where" does the information on the site come from? What information is being provided, and where that information comes from? Students can examine whether the site includes primary as well as secondary source information, and how that information is provided to readers and viewers—as static presentations of facts or interactive explorations that require thoughtful examination and analysis.
5. "Why" is this site and its information better, more useful, or more reliable than information on other sites? How do students make informed judgments about which sites are credible resources for academic study and which ones are not? Students decide if the information presented contributes to a more complete understanding of the histories of events, people, or societies while assessing if the site's organization will invite other students to interact with the resources for school classes or personal learning experiences.

Students readily understand how the five Ws provide them with questions to ask to evaluate a site's credibility and reliability as a teaching and learning resource. Many teachers follow a rule that a site should be used as a source of academic information only when students can answer all of the five Ws without doubts about its credibility. And, as they examine the "who, what, when, where, and why" of a site, students learn how meanings and messages are communicated online.

UNRELIABLE RESOURCES AND THEIR CHARACTERISTICS

What makes an online resource unsuitable for classroom learning activities or inclusion on teacher- and student-made educational wikis? Websites to avoid have one or more of the following characteristics: (1) excessive advertising; (2) off-topic links; (3) fake news, overt bias, or hidden points of view; and (4) inaccessible content presentations.

Excessive Advertising

Advertising for products and services is a prominent feature of many websites; it is a primary way that a site makes money for its creators. Ads for products and services come in varied formats—videos that play before content can be seen; pictures, posters, and banners arranged up and down the sides of pages; pop-up boxes that appear in the middle of paragraphs; and other product placement strategies. Some ads present extravagant claims for improving health, making large amount of money, or viewing celebrities in compromising situations.

Encountering online ads, web-savvy adults scan past them, focusing on finding the content they came to read. For younger readers, the result of viewing online ads can be quite different. They tend to look at the ads. There is a "revolution in the world of advertising and marketing to children and teens," observed the consumer watchdog organization Common Sense Media (2014, p. 16), estimating that youngsters aged two to eleven see 25,600 ads per year on television and an untold number more online. Nearly four out of five of children's most popular websites (87 percent) have some form of advertising and this "encompasses not only more sophisticated and enticing banner ads but also 'advergames,' online videos, branded websites, virtual worlds and social marketing" (p. 9).

American Medical Association researchers found children and adolescents view an average of 40,000 ads a year between TV, the web, movies, billboards, and magazines (Committee on Communications, 2006). Children aged eight and younger, the researchers noted, are "cognitively and psychologically defenseless" against an avalanche of ads being predisposed to accept published claims as truth. Tweens and teens are also susceptible to unsubstantiated product statements and exploitative marketing campaigns.

General academic information sites such as History.com, About.com, Infoplease.com, Britannica.com, or Eyewitness to History.com include multiple ads on their pages as do the websites of newspapers and for-profit history and humanities-themed organizations. Many of these sites employ built-in tracking tools that "customize" ads while collecting data about a computer user's browsing history. Such ads blur the lines between academic information and product sales. Like the Stanford University study cited earlier in this chapter, researchers in England found that two-thirds of eight- to fifteen-year-olds could not differentiate between paid advertisements or sponsored links and actual results on a search page (Ofcom, 2015, p. 8).

Contrastingly, multiple online sources of academic information are ad-free or limit the number of ads to mainly education-related products and services. Ads on some websites can be eliminated through paid subscriptions. As a rule, teachers and students can try to use as their preferred source of curriculum-related information only sites without excessive advertising.

Off-Topic Links

Another complication occurs when sites containing useful academic information also display hyperlinks to sites unrelated to the topic being studied. Known as "clickbait" and alternately called "Around the Web," "From the Web," "Sponsored Content," or "Trending," these links take readers to off-topic photos, slideshows, videos, and promotional appeals related to celebrity lifestyles, sexually themed behaviors, supposedly revolutionary but unproven medical treatments, strategies for instantly improving personal finances, and other nonacademic materials. Such links divert students away from an intended focus of learning as they click from one enticingly presented off-topic choice to another.

Educational psychologists refer to this potential for distraction as a problem of cognitive overload. In any situation, learners can only process so much information at one time before they begin missing key points, becoming frustrated, or deciding to abandon an activity before completion as they experience cognitive overload.

Cognitive overload can seriously disrupt classroom learning, for as educators Richard E. Mayer and Roxana Moreno (2003, pp. 43, 50) have noted: To achieve "meaningful learning" and "deep understanding," students need to attend to the "important aspects of the presented material, mentally organizing it into a coherent cognitive structure, and integrating it with relevant existing learning." In digital learning contexts where students must attend to words and pictures (and moving images and online links in the case of websites), cognitive overload occurs when there is too much information for anyone to process reasonably. In Mayer and Moreno's view, teachers must design instruction "in ways that minimize any unnecessary cognitive load."

Off-topic links appear on many general information and popular media sites like Time, Huffington Post, and Slate as well as the websites for newspapers, magazines, and commercial television stations. At the same time, some online news sites like the *New York Times* and NPR (National Public Radio) feature links that are related to the news stories on a page. Teachers and students can evaluate online sites and avoid those that offer information distraction. Teachers can also teach students about off-topics links and cognitive overload so that they learn to be critical readers and viewers of web page materials.

There are times when the educational value of the online learning material cancels the potential distraction and overload from off-topic links on a page. One telling example is a World War II retrospective at *Atlantic.com* featuring photographs taken by Ansel Adams at the Manzanar War Relocation Center between 1943 and 1944. The images are from the Library of Congress, but *The Atlantic* has assembled them in an easily accessible online slideshow. In a case of a learning resource such as this, teachers and students can choose to ignore the off-topic links on the page to view this unique progression of historical images.

Fake News, Overt Bias, and Hidden Points of View

Fake news, bias, and hidden points of view are an ever-present online problem where organizations and individuals can freely express opinions and viewpoints that are not grounded in historical or scientific facts. Bias comes in many forms. There is overt or direct bias where a website, chain e-mail, or social media post explicitly sets forth a political point of view or seeks to promote a social or economic agenda. And there is less obvious, hidden bias where those same sources conceal rather than reveal their primary perspectives or point of views.

Two researchers from the media watchdog site FactCheck.org have listed what they call the "key characteristics of bogusness" found in chain e-mails and social media posts (Robertson, 2014; Robertson & Kiely, 2016). First, authors are either anonymous or supposedly famous persons whose words can be trusted without checking. Second, there are recurring features of the sites: spelling errors, lots of capital letters, an overuse of exclamation points at the end of sentences, and reassurances that the message is not a hoax. Third, there are references to legitimate sources, that when investigated, contradict the information in the e-mail or post. There are also mathematical or numerical claims that prove false and misleading when investigated closely. Fact-checking and critical evaluation tools are needed to combat fake news and bias information that is growing increasingly sophisticated in its online presentation.

Being able to determine the accuracy, bias, and/or point of view of websites, e-mails, and social media posts is essential to digital literacy learning.

As an example of how bias detection can function, consider the ways that different websites explore the connections between the Little Ice Age in Europe, the Great Famine of 1315–1317, and the bubonic plague (or Black Death), three world history curriculum topics relevant to understanding life in the Middle Ages, as well as modern-day debates about pandemics, global warming, and climate change. For historians, the poverty and poor health brought on by the Great Famine were critical factors in the onset of Bubonic Plague while the Great Famine resulted in part from the onset of the Little Ice Age, a period of global cooling that began altering the crop-growing seasons around 1300 (McNeil, 1998).

Looking online for resources about the Little Ice Age, the Great Famine, and the Black Death, teachers and students will immediately find materials posted by university organizations (Scripps Institute of Oceanography at the University of California San Diego), government agencies (National Oceanic and Atmospheric Administration), science magazines (Discover, Earth/Sky), and independent researchers (ranging from *Skeptical Science* maintained by John Cook, a climate communication fellow at the Global Change Institute at the University of Queensland in Australia that seeks to provide "what peer reviewed research has to say about global warming" to *American Thinker*, a site that regularly publishes extreme right-wing science writing with an emphasis on creationism and climate change denial).

As the Little Ice Age example shows, because bias is not always overt, it comes in many forms. Every possible information source must be evaluated by assessing accuracy, authority, objectivity, currency, coverage, and relevancy. Learning how to distinguish reliable materials from bogus claims unsubstantiated by factual evidence is part of how constructing educational wikis teaches the skills of Internet research and digital literacy.

Resources to use to identify high-quality sites for academic learning and wiki construction include the following:

- *FactCheck.org* from the Annenberg Public Policy Center, University of Pennsylvania monitors the factual accuracy of the news; its *Viral Spiral* section tracks online rumors with links to legitimate articles debunking false claims.
- Other resources for locating reliable online information include *Politifact*, *OpenSecrets.org* from the Center for Responsive Politics; *Right Wing Watch* from People for the American Way; the Pew Internet Research Project; *FAIR (Fairness & Accuracy in Reporting)*; and The Center for News Literacy at Stony Brook University.

Inaccessible Content Presentations

Online resources vary in the level of accessibility. Some sites present information in a formal, academic style; others have informal and graphical modes of presentation. Websites with differing reading formats are then accessed by students who bring their own widely varying reading skills to the material. The result is a complex set of interactions between texts and readers with the potential for mismatches between a website's reading level and the language comprehension skills of student readers.

For any academic topic, there are sites whose reading level can be far beyond or considerably below the reading skills of students. A site featuring primary source materials or one that offers lengthy text essays by historians usually presents comprehension challenges for even the strongest readers in a high school class while being mostly inaccessible for most middle or elementary school students. By contrast, a site that presents information in a newspaper article-like format might be oversimplified for strong high school student readers, but accessible for younger readers. Matching reading accessibility of online resources to the readers of educational wikis needs constant consideration. One resource is Newsela, a free website that provides versions of current news stories written for different levels of reading comprehension.

In 2010, Google announced it was offering a reading level filter that allowed users to annotate search results as basic, intermediate, or advanced. In theory, this feature would enable teachers to tailor web content to the reading skills of students. Although Google discontinued the filter in 2015, there are sites that will calculate a readability score for web material: *JuicyStudio, Readability Test Tool, Readability.info, Text Content Analysis, SMOG Readability Calculator,* and *Lexicool Textalyser* use mathematical formulas to determine the years of schooling needed to understand web content as well as the overall ease of a site's online reading experience. While these types of scores provide only a general assessment, teachers and students can collaboratively determine whether a site offers a reading experience that advances or limits knowledge and understanding of history and literature topics.

For comprehension, it is helpful to limit the inclusion of sites featuring lengthy text-based descriptions of topics. Wikipedia has a page on the Irish Potato Famine (an often-discussed event in the context of European immigration to the United States before the Civil War) that is nearly 14,000 words in length, including footnotes. The combination of page length and academic writing make it inaccessible for all but a few student readers.

At the same time, wiki page builders may want to include links to lengthy primary source materials (e.g., full-text links to Shakespeare's plays,

Machiavelli's *The Prince*, or other influential literature and important documents) so readers can access the entire source. In these instances, teachers can summarize the material and discuss sections of the text with students.

SELECT/CONSIDER/REJECT EVALUATIONS

Evaluating web resources can be done qualitatively or quantitatively. Educational technologist Kathy Schrock poses a series of questions—phrased differently for elementary, middle, and high school students—that require Yes/No answers about the technical and visual features, content, author, and publisher of a page. Students then expand their Yes/No answers by writing short narrative summaries about why a site should or should not be used as a resource for in-class or online teaching and learning.

Other web page evaluators use rubrics with point totals to numerically separate reliable from less reliable resources. A site from the University of Wisconsin Stout assigns points for criteria ranging from exemplary, proficient, partially proficient, and unsatisfactory while the Sacramento State University's system makes its evaluation criteria exemplary, effective and needs improvement. Ohio's Solon City School District assigns points ranging from exemplary to competent, developing, or unsatisfactory.

In deciding what resources to post on a wiki, we use a variation of Kathy Schrock's qualitative approach where students submit their own written decisions about whether to select, consider, or reject a page for classroom and wiki learning activities.

- "Select" refers to a site that offers credible and reliable academic information, usually from historical organizations, museums, government agencies, and mainstream media outlets.
- "Consider" means the site has useful academic information but also has features that may limit its usefulness for teaching and learning; teachers and students need to carefully consider whether to use it or not as part of learning activities.
- "Reject" is reserved for sites that do not contribute to improved knowledge and understanding due to commercialization, off-topic links, bias, or inaccessible reading levels. These sites would not be used unless no other alternative exists for accessing the information online.

The following two topics illustrate the Select/Consider/Reject approach in action: the Viking Exploration of North America from an upper elementary and middle school curriculum and the Irish Potato Famine for high school students.

Sample Page: Viking Exploration of North America

> Visit the *Viking Exploration of North America*:
> https://resourcesforhistoryteachers.wikispaces.com/5.1

The *Viking Exploration of North America* is based on a 5th-grade learning standard: "Describe the earliest explorations of the New World by the Vikings, the period and locations of their explorations, and the evidence for them" (Massachusetts Department of Education, 2003, p. 28). Beginning with the keywords "Viking discovery of North America" and "Leif Eriksson," we used Google to generate a list of possible sites and then decided which ones to include in the *resourcesforhistoryteachers* wiki (see Table 3.1).

Table 3.1.   Select/Consider/Reject Decisions for the *Viking Exploration of North America* wiki Page

Select	Source: *Discovering North America*
	Author: Smithsonian National Museum of Natural History
	Source: *The Vikings, 800 to 1066*
	Author: BBC History
	Source: *Vikings*
	Author: e-Themes, University of Missouri
	Source: *The Vikings*
	Author: NOVA Online
	Source: *The Little Ice Age in Europe*
	Author: Suffolk County (New York) Community College
	Source: *L'Anse aux Meadows*: UNESCO World Heritage Site in Newfoundland, Canada
	Author: Video posted on YouTube by Explore Canada
	Source: *Proclamation 3610: Leif Erikson Day, 1964*
	Author: American Presidency Project
Consider	Source: *How to Make a Ship for a School Project*
	Author: e-How.com
	Source: *Leif Eriksson*
	Author: Greenland.com
	Source: *Leif Eriksson*
	Author: Metropolitan News Company.net
Reject	Source: *Leif Eriksson Biographies*
	Authors: Eyewitness to History.com, Softpedia.com, Discovery.com, Indian Country Today Media Network.com, History.com
	Source: *Vikings Arms and Armor*
	Author: Hurstwic.org, a Viking Combat Training organization
	Source: *More Proof That Vikings Were First to America*
	Author: Time.com

Sites from the Smithsonian National Museum of Natural History, BBC History, the University of Missouri, NOVA Online, Suffolk County Community College, Explore Canada, and the American Presidency Project were placed in the Select category. Each of these (a) was authored by scholars or staff associated with an academic, historical, or media organization; (b) had been vetted and then updated recently (the BBC site was archived in 2011); and (c) was offered analysis of the historical evidence that Viking explorers reached North America beginning in the tenth century.

"How to Make a Ship for a School Project" from *ehow.com*, a do-it-yourself home improvement website was placed in the Consider category. The project idea is interesting, but the website included many advertisements as well as multiple links to off-topic sites. While this might be an informative site for teachers, it seemed less useful for students who might be distracted by the off-topic materials. Leif Eriksson biography sites from Greenland.com and Metropolitan News Company were similarly placed in the Consider category. Greenland.com had interesting photographs, but the site itself promotes travel and tourism in the country. The Metropolitan News site had a lengthy text biography that would be understandable by only the most fluent student readers.

The Reject group included dot.com general history information sites including Eyewitness to History.com, Softpedia.com, Discovery.com, Indian Country Today.com, Media Network.com, and History.com. All of these sites contain multiple ads, off-topic links, and static presentations of information. The site *Vikings Arms and Armor* was rejected because it is maintained by a combat training business and featured a more militaristic than historical presentation of content. The Time.com site had useful information, but the page was filled with ads and off-topic links.

Sample Example: The Irish Potato Famine

> Visit the *Irish Potato Famine* page:
> https://resourcesforhistoryteachers.wikispaces.com/Irish+Potato+Famine

The *Irish Potato Famine* page is based on a subtopic in the Massachusetts curriculum standard "Explain the causes and impact of the wave of immigration from Northern Europe to America in the 1840s and 1850s" (Massachusetts Department of Education, 2003, p. 69). The Potato Famine is also a subtopic in Advanced Placement (AP) World History Key Concept 5.4: Global Migration (1750–1900).

After entering "Irish Potato Famine" as a keyword for a Google search and listing the websites found on the first three pages of search results, the following Select/Consider/Reject determinations were made about which resources to link on the *resourcesforhistoryteachers* wiki as credible teaching and learning resources.

Three research-based sites from universities were placed in the Select category: a summary of the potato famine from *Digital History* from the University of Houston; "Interpreting the Irish Famine, 1846–1850" with primary source materials from the University of Virginia; and "Monoculture and the Irish Potato Famine: Cases of Missing Genetic Variation," a scientific analysis of the famine from *Understanding Evolution*, a site at the University of California Berkeley. An article "Scientists Finally Pinpoint the Pathogen That Caused the Irish Potato Famine" from Smithsonian Magazine was also included. Although the Smithsonian site has ads for newspapers and magazines, the research is up-to-date and compellingly presented.

Materials from BBC History and the Victorian web were also selected as reliable summaries of the famine and its consequences, both in Europe and the Americas. Two multimedia resources: the Irish Potato Famine Documentary on YouTube that combines music, pictures, and text (without any voice over) and the Irish Potato Famine on Vimeo that presents an animated view of the event were also added to the page.

"In a Nutshell: The Irish Potato Famine" from HistoryExtra.com was placed in the Consider category since it provided a succinct summary in an easy-to-understand question/answer format despite having multiple ads on the page. "The Irish Potato Famine of the 1840s" from VintageVeggies. com, a site sponsored by the Victory Seed Company, was also a site worth considering. Although the page does link to sites for buying seed products, the article thoughtfully explores how an overreliance on a single potato crop variety set the stage for the famine.

The Reject group included dot.com general history information sites including Eyewitness to History, the History Place, and History Learning Site. Each contained multiple ads, off-topic links, and static presentations of information. The Mises Institute site was rejected based on its overt political expression of free market economics and private property. HenryMakow.com was blocked on our university's server as a hate site and thus was rejected for inclusion on the wiki.

BUILDING A COLLECTION OF RELIABLE RESOURCES

Building a classroom-based collection of reliable resources is an effective way for teachers and students to locate high-quality web resources for use on

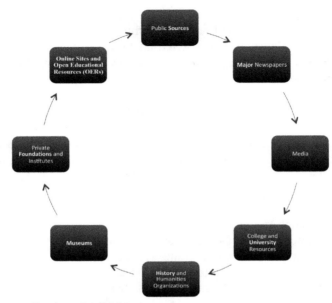

Figure 3.1.   Collection of Reliable Resources

educational wiki pages and in classroom learning. The first step is to identify where to go online to locate websites that feature high-quality, accurate,
vetted, student-accessible learning resources. Figure 3.1 shows the reliable
resources collection used in constructing pages on the *resourcesforhistoryteachers, Teaching Resources for English* and *Teaching Geography* wikis.
   The collection's categories include:

- **Public Sources** are publicly funded sites such as the Library of Congress,
  National Archives, Presidential Libraries, National Park Service, and
  resources such as the National Endowment for the Humanities; the Office
  of the Historian, U.S. Department of State; or the World Factbook from the
  Central Intelligence Agency. State and local government sites and public
  libraries are also included in this category.
- **Major Newspapers** are highly regarded news sources of record that feature
  authoritative and trustworthy reporting; for example, the *New York Times,
  Washington Post, Wall Street Journal, Los Angeles Times, The Economist,*
  and *The Guardian* (United Kingdom).
- **Media and Social Media** are online information outlets offering videos,
  podcasts, tweets, blogs, discussion forums, and interactive websites including NPR (National Public Radio), PBS (Public Broadcasting Service) and
  PBS Learning Media, BBC (British Broadcasting Company), History Channel, YouTube, Discovery Channel, TED Talks, Vimeo, and Kahn Academy.
  This category also includes educational groups and teacher learning communities such as those found on social bookmarking sites such as Diigo.

- **College and University Sources** are materials from academic departments, libraries, and institutes. Examples include The American Presidency Project, Miller Center of Public Affairs, University of Virginia; Chinese Railroad Workers Project, Stanford University; FactCheck.org, Annenberg Public Policy Center, University of Pennsylvania; The Martin Luther King, Jr. Center for Nonviolent Social Change, Stanford University; Global Nonviolent Action Database, Swarthmore College; and The Choices Program, Brown University.
- **History and Humanities Organizations** are sites devoted to history and humanities learning, including the National Council for the Social Studies, National Council of Teachers of English, National Center for History in the Schools, American Historical Society, National Council for History Education, ALA (American Library Association), Gilder Lehrman Institute of American History, National Geographic, National Humanities Center, Poetry Foundation, Roy Rosenzweig Center for History and New Media, and state and local historical societies.
- **Museums** include institutions that collect and display objects and materials of cultural, historical, scientific, and artistic importance such as, Smithsonian Institution, Metropolitan Museum of Art, Museum of Fine Art, the British Museum, National Women's History Museum, National Museum of African American History and Culture, and American Writers Museum. Museums and websites of notable writers and playwrights are also part of this category.
- **Foundations and Institutes** are think tanks and research centers whose mission is to explore historical and contemporary topics; for example, Pew Research Center, Annenberg Public Policy Center, American Civil Liberties Union, GLSEN, Digital Public Library of America, Brookings Institution, and Anti-Defamation League.
- **Online and Open Educational Resources (OERs)** include organizations that post teaching and learning materials for the history and humanities education. Online sites include Zinn Education Project, National History Education Clearinghouse, National Center for History in the Schools, Internet History Sourcebooks Project, Google World Wonders Project, UNESCO World Heritage Centre, and The Writer's Almanac with Garrison Keillor. Open Educational Resources (OERs) that teachers and students can freely use, revise, and redistribute are also part of this category, including Wikimedia Commons, OER Commons, Curriki, EDSITEment, Open Stax College, and Smithsonian Learning Lab.

Once a collection of resources is in place, students can then engage in completing the following steps of a Select/Consider/Reject evaluation:

- Review as a class the "who, what, when, where and why" of website evaluation and the four categories of online resources to avoid (excessive ads, off-topic links, bias point of view, inaccessible content).

- Select a topic from a district, state or national curriculum standard or choose people or events that students need or want to learn about even if it is not specifically mentioned in a curriculum framework.
- Brainstorm as a group search terms to use with Google or another search engine to research the assigned topic.
- Have students review each site that appears on the first or second page of search results, dividing the sites into one of three Select/Consider/Reject categories using the constellation of reliable resources as a guide.
- Have students provide a written evaluation of why they would select, consider, or reject a site as a resource for linking on a class wiki or using for in-class learning activities along with an assessment of each of the five Ws of website evaluation.
- Give the same curriculum topic or learning standard to more than one student researcher or research team so individuals and groups can compare their evaluations and reach a consensus about whether to select, consider, or reject.

As Select, Consider, or Reject evaluators, students become digitally literate researchers and curators of history and humanities content. Working individually or in cooperative learning groups, students review choices and make selections about resources to post for online or in-class activities. Analyzing web resources, students learn multimodally by reading, listening, and viewing multiple websites. As they report what they have learned, they practice summarizing the histories and stories of people and events.

Consulting resources other than Wikipedia and exploring more than the first page of search engine results, students discover the variety and complexity of online resources. They notice the differences in content and presentation between dot.com, dot.org, and dot.edu sites. They recognize the importance of identifying the author(s) of online material and assessing the background of individuals and organizations relative to a topic.

As critical evaluators of online content, student researchers teach themselves literacy reasoning skills by explaining why a resource should be included on a wiki page or used as a class learning activity. They begin to think critically when listening to counter arguments for why a resource might not be an accurate or useful learning material. Finally, as they engage in online research and website evaluation, students begin uncovering and discovering the hidden histories and untold stories of African Americans, Latinos, Native Americans, women and LGBTQ individuals and groups, integral participants in the history and humanities curriculum, and the focus of the book's next chapter.

Chapter 4

Uncovering Hidden Histories and Untold Stories

In 1945, nearly a decade before the historic 1954 *Brown v. Board of Education* Supreme Court decision, Sylvia Mendez, a Mexican American 3rd grader living in Los Angeles, California, was denied admission to the white-only public elementary school near her home. Sylvia's parents filed a class action suit in U.S. District Court along with a group of other Mexican American families contending that the school district's policy of segregating students by ancestry violated the equal protection clause of the Fourteenth Amendment. The subsequent court case, *Mendez v. Westminster,* established precedents that informed the Brown decision seven years later. As the district court judge wrote in his decision in favor of the families: "A paramount requisite in the American system of public education is social equality. It must be open to all children by unified school association regardless of lineage."

Despite its precedence-setting position in the struggle for civil rights and school desegregation, the Mendez case is not widely known nor prominently discussed in school textbooks, state curriculum frameworks, or teacher lesson plans. Yet the stories surrounding the case are dramatic, compelling moments in America's history. The class action suit was filed on behalf of some 5,000 persons of Mexican descent. Earl Warren was governor of California at the time of the case and Chief Justice of the Supreme Court when the Brown decision was rendered. Thurgood Marshall, writing a friend of the court brief for the National Association for the Advancement of Colored People (NAACP), set forth arguments about the harmful impacts of educational segregation that would be the basis for the Brown decision. In 2007, the U.S. Post Office issued a stamp commemorating the *Mendez v. Westminster* decision; Sylvia Mendez received the Presidential Medal of Freedom in 2011.

Mendez v. Westminster introduces the importance of wikis presenting hidden histories and untold stories in history and humanities classes. Hidden histories and untold stories refer to people and events that have been omitted from textbooks and curriculum frameworks, including women's history; the histories of people of color; history of the working classes and immigrants; and the histories of LGBTQ individuals and groups.

Wikis, collaboratively built by students and teachers, expand the scope of standards and curriculum by revealing hidden histories and untold stories as essential features of history and humanities teaching and learning. The chapter begins by explaining how current state history standards limit whose history will be taught in schools. Next, hidden histories and untold stories are proposed as ways to enable students to discover and uncover information integral to understanding and expanding school curriculum. Finally, the chapter shows ways to present people and events from African American, women's, and LGBTQ history by connecting hidden histories to often-told stories, enlarging the curriculum while contrasting multicultural content with prevailing textbook narratives.

WHOSE HISTORY IN STATE CURRICULUM FRAMEWORKS

Every state has its own K–12 history/social studies learning standards. You can locate them at the "Browse State Standards" section of *Teachinghistory. org* from the National History Education Clearinghouse, online at http:// teachinghistory.org/teaching-materials/state-standards. These frameworks are lengthy documents, outlining what students are supposed to know and be able to do at every grade level. Learning goals are framed around large topics and expansive time periods, as in the following examples:

- A South Carolina standard about colonial North America before the American Revolution asks high school students to "Summarize the distinct characteristics of each colonial region in the settlement and development of British North America, including religious, social, political, and economic differences" (South Carolina Department of Education)
- A Colorado middle school civics standard expects students to be able to "Describe instances in which major political, social, economic, or cultural changes occurred and the reasons for the changes" (Colorado Department of Education)
- A 7th-grade Minnesota economics standard directs students to "Describe how the interaction of buyers (through demand) and sellers (through supply) determines price in a market" (Minnesota Department of Education, 2013)

Finding historical and contemporary examples to address these standards in ways that students will find interesting and relevant is an ongoing challenge for teachers.

As statements of educational policy, standards generate controversy and dispute. At every grade level, there are more topics to teach than time to teach them. Decisions must be made about what content to address and what topics to leave out of the curriculum. Competing political interest groups also seek to influence these content coverage decisions, insisting that certain material be emphasized while other material is minimized or eliminated. These disagreements involve educators, families, community members, and policymakers in debates over whose history will be taught in schools.

Through multiple aspects of the educational experience, including curriculum, every state and local district seeks to affirm respect for the race, color, sex, gender identity, religion, national origin, and sexual orientation of students, teachers, school staff, and community members. But even though policy frameworks and mission statements support diversity as an educational goal, students and teachers are still faced with the task of locating the histories and stories that will reveal the lived experiences of both women and men as well as all ethnic and cultural groups in historically accurate terms.

Integrating hidden histories and untold stories makes academic learning real for students by revealing the conflicts, suspense, and drama of the past—bringing alive the complexities and oppressions faced by individuals and groups. By contrast, most history textbooks, argued historian James W. Loewen (2007, p. 6), treat the past as a simple morality play where social problems arise, get resolved, and then disappear from the historical narrative—an approach that fails to engage "students of color, children of working-class families, girls who notice the dearth of female historical figures, or members of any group that has not achieved socioeconomic success."

FINDING WHAT HAS BEEN HIDDEN

State curriculum frameworks are imprecise guides to multicultural history. Sometimes a state framework will offer diverse history topics within the text of a standard while in other states a similar standard is phrased more broadly and less inclusively. New York's U.S. history standard on the growth of industrialization and urbanization in years between the Civil War and World War I directly references the experiences of women and African American reformers, stating that students should "trace the reform efforts" of the time, including

- Jane Addams and Hull House;
- Jacob Riis and his book, *How the Other Half Lives*;
- then Governor Theodore Roosevelt and the Tenement Reform Commission;
- Upton Sinclair's book *The Jungle* and the Meat Inspection Act;
- Margaret Sanger and birth control movement;

- Ida Tarbell's book *The History of the Standard Oil Company*;
- Ida B. Wells' efforts to stop lynching of African Americans; and
- Booker T. Washington's founding of the Tuskegee Institute (The State Education Department and The University of the State of New York, 2015).

By contrast, Nevada's standard for the same time period states teachers and students should "describe the effects of industrialization and new technologies on the development of the United States" (p. 8) while South Carolina's standards direct students to "compare the accomplishments and limitations of the women's suffrage movement and the Progressive Movement in affecting social and political reforms in America, including the roles of the media and of reformers such as Carrie Chapman Catt, Alice Paul, Jane Addams, and presidents Theodore Roosevelt and Woodrow Wilson." The Advanced Placement U.S. History framework for this historical period is similarly broad in scope; its Key Concept 6.3 states: "The Gilded Age produced new cultural and intellectual movements, public reform efforts, and political debates over economic and social policies." The AP U.S. framework references by name only Jane Addams and her work in settlement houses.

Whether or not mandated learning standards include references to or provide guidance for teaching multiculturally, wiki page building serves as opportunities for students and teachers to become investigators of hidden histories/untold stories. Starting with the text of a standard, students and teachers can first explore what textbooks and other sources discuss about the topics in the standard. Then researching paper and digital sources, they find histories and stories that uncover broader historical narratives for inclusion in class-made wikis and classroom learning activities.

Annie Cobb, the first person processed through the Ellis Island Immigration Station on January 1, 1892, offers an example of a hidden history story. She had been long memorialized as an immigrant who pursued the American Dream, coming to a new land as a teenager, moving west to Texas to marry and begin a family, only to die tragically in a streetcar accident. There are statutes of her on both sides of the Atlantic, one in Cobh, Ireland and the other at Ellis Island. However, that story is not entirely true. She did arrive in New York City from Ireland at age fifteen, but she did not go west to Texas. Instead she lived a poor immigrant's life on New York's Lower East Side, marrying a baker, giving birth to eleven children (only five of whom lived to adulthood) and dying of a heart attack at age forty-seven (Roberts, 2006).

Students can read about Annie Cobb's life in online materials from the Ellis Island Foundation and learn how one genealogist tracked down the actual story of her life. They can view photographs of her seaside statutes, listen to song lyrics about her story, and hear a podcast about her life in America. They can expand their knowledge by taking the "Lower Eastside

Tenement Virtual Tour," playing "From Ellis Island to Orchard Street," an online game from the Tenement Museum, and reading primary sources about immigrant experience. Finally, students can debate whether or not her life epitomized the despair and poverty of immigrant experience in urban industrial American society.

There are multiple sources for teachers and students to use to locate missing and long-neglected histories and stories, starting with notable history books that explore the experiences of diverse peoples: *A People's History of the United States: 1492—Present*, Howard Zinn (2015); *A Different Mirror: A History of Multicultural America*, Ronald Takaki (2008); *Born for Liberty*, Sara Evans (1997); *Harvest of Empire*: *A History of Latinos in America*, Juan Gonzalez (2011); *An Indigenous Peoples' History of the United States*, Roxanne Dunbar-Ortiz (2014); *A Queer History of the United States*, Michael Bronski (2011).

Notable world history titles include *1493: Uncovering the World Columbus Created* and *1491: New Revelations of the Americas Before Columbus*, Charles C. Mann (2005, 2011); *The World That Trade Created: Society, Culture and the World Economy, 1400—the Present*, Kenneth Pomeranz & Steven Topik (2005); *Empires of Food: Feast, Famine and the Rise and Fall of Civilizations*, Evan D. Fraser & Andrew Rimas (2010). *Lost Discoveries: The Ancient Roots of Modern Science—from the Babylonians to the Maya*, Dick Teresi (2002); *Pathfinders: A Global History of Exploration*, Felipe Fernandez-Armesto (2007); and *Children of the Days: A Calendar of Human History*, Edward Galeano (2013).

In addition to print books, online resources propel the search for hidden histories and untold stories. Text Box 4.1 offers an initial list of sources to consult. Many of these organizations will also send e-mail alerts when new material is published.

TEXT BOX 4.1

Online Sources of Hidden History/Untold Story Resources

"If We Only Knew Our History," Zinn Education Project, has articles that explore the topics major textbooks ignore.

"The Writer's Almanac," American Public Media, provides short biographies and event summaries for each day of the year.

"TeachingHistory.org," from the Roy Rosenzweig Center for History and New Media, George Mason University has extensive history and humanities curriculum resources for all grade levels.

"Heritage Teaching Resources," Smithsonian Education has curriculum-related materials for teaching black history, women's history, Asian Pacific American history, Hispanic heritage, and American Indian heritage.

"OpenSecrets.org" from the Center for Responsive Politics tracks the impact of money in politics.

"FactCheck.org" from the Annenberg Public Policy Center monitors the factual accuracy of statements by political figures.

"National Priorities Project" offers information about federal government spending.

"Center for American Women and Politics," Rutgers University, conducts research on women's participation in politics.

"History Detectives Special Investigations" from PBS explores long-standing mysteries from American history.

"Books That Shaped America," Library of Congress, features important American literature from 1750 to 2000.

"Notable Social Studies Trade Books for Young People," National Council for the Social Studies, lists picture books and young adult literature that addresses diverse cultures and experiences.

"Notable Children's Books," Association for Library Service to Children, lists the best stories of the year for younger, middle, and older readers.

PBS produces amazing shows addressing well-known and little-known people and events. Many of these shows have companion websites with materials for classroom learning. Teachers and students can search PBS by genre (history, culture, news & public affairs, science & nature) to find topics to investigate.

Newspaper and online obituaries are another ways for teachers and students to explore the intersections between a person's life and wider historical events and trends. When the Chinese American animator Tyrus Wong died in late 2016 at the age of 106, his obituary presented opportunities to explore his art (the animations he did for the Disney movie *Bambi* drew inspiration from Song Dynasty paintings) and his life (he was detained at the Angel Island Immigration Station in San Francisco before being allowed to enter the country and then had to overcome anti-Chinese discrimination, fueled by the Chinese Exclusion Act of 1882, before becoming one of the twentieth century's most celebrated artists).

Exploring hidden histories and untold stories supports Howard Zinn's goal of providing students with a "more accurate, complex and engaging understanding of United States history than is found in traditional textbooks and curricula" (Zinn Education Project, 2016). But, as Bill Bigelow (2008, p. 3) stated: "A people's history requires a people's pedagogy to match." Students need to understand "history as a series of choices and turning points-junctures at which ordinary people interpreted social conditions and took actions that made a difference." As they use wikis to enlarge views of the past, students and teachers are better able to understand how present-day choices will shape everyone's futures.

COVER, DISCOVER, AND UNCOVER PEOPLE AND EVENTS

A first step in making hidden histories and untold stories central to learning happens in how teachers and students go about "covering," "discovering" and "uncovering" history and humanities curriculum topics.

- "Cover" refers to conveying the academic content of state and local curriculum frameworks to students.
- "Discover" describes exploring academic topics multimodally through reading, viewing, listening, and interacting with online resources.
- "Uncover" means integrating the experiences of diverse individuals and groups into history and humanities learning.

Cover, discover, and uncover form a connected framework for using classroom wikis to integrate hidden histories and untold stories into the teaching of standards and curriculum.

Covering Curriculum and Standards

Covering the required curriculum has long been the center of history teaching in K–12 schools (Cuban, 2016, 1993). This approach "casts the professor (and his or her chosen texts) in the role of historical authority, with students assigned the task of absorbing and reproducing expert knowledge" (Sipress & Voelker, 2011, p. 1050). Underlying the coverage model is the assumption that students need to have a general knowledge about U.S. and world history, and the best way to do this is through survey courses at secondary and college levels.

Discovering Curriculum and Standards

Discovering means populating wiki pages with multimodal learning resources—pictorial and visual images as well as links to film and video resources, maps and timelines, learning games, simulations, and visualizations and inquiry-learning websites—an approach supported by research in the science of learning. This "contemporary view of learning" called constructivism, noted the editors of the influential *How People Learn* series, emphasizes that learners construct new knowledge through active engagement with meaningful puzzles and problems (National Research Council, 2000).

From a constructivist perspective, discovering knowledge happens when teachers challenge students' taken-for-granted assumptions through inquiry-based, multimodal problem solving activities. Studying the Civil War, students might learn about Abraham Lincoln's Gettysburg Address, a seminal document of American freedom by first reading the primary source text. A multimodal exploration could begin by watching a segment on the Address from Ken Burns' Civil War PBS series and then viewing everyday Americans from teens to octogenarians reciting Lincoln's words on the website, "Learn the Address."

To continue discovering the Gettysburg Address, students and teachers can visit an interactive online exhibit from the Library of Congress; compare the text of the five existing copies on the Gettysburg Battlefield website; view an interactive map of the battle from the Smithsonian; and watch a tour of the battlefield from the Gilder Lehrman Institute of American History. Multimodal resources enliven text-based descriptions of Lincoln's speech while enabling learners to construct their own understandings of the Address, its importance to the Union war effort, and its enduring legacy as a document of American freedom.

Uncovering Curriculum and Standards

Uncovering history and humanities content is derived from term "uncoverage," an approach outlined in a 2006 article by historian Lendol Calder in the *Journal of American History*. Calder urged teachers to have students act like investigating historians, not memorizers of factual information. Instead of facts-first, coverage-based instructional approaches where students' role is to recall information for the test, but much of what is then forgotten over time,

> We should be designing classroom environments that expose the very things hidden away by traditional survey instruction: the linchpin ideas of historical inquiry that are not obvious or easily comprehended; the inquiries, arguments, assumptions, and points of view that make knowledge what it is for practitioners of our discipline; the cognitive contours of history as an epistemological domain (Calder, 2006, p. 1363)

Uncovering engages students in inquiry learning (Wiggins & McTighe, 2005). In inquiry learning, "questions—rather than answers—drive instruction" (Lesh, 2011, p. 18). Exploring historical time periods, events, and historical persons, students find questions they want to answer. They gather evidence from primary sources and secondary accounts. They analyze sources to develop historical interpretations, remain ready to revise those views when additional evidence is found, and function like historians while developing habits of mind that emphasize inquiry-thinking skills.

In an uncoverage approach, the textbook itself is a source to be analyzed rather than a collection of information to be remembered for the test. Teacher Bill Bigelow (n.d., p. 4) uses textbooks to have students "explore the politics of print" and to recognize that the task of each reader is "to comprehend what is written, but also to question why it is written." He believes students and teachers must access wide-ranging historical learning materials, from different types of primary sources to numerous and competing secondary accounts of people and events.

Sam Wineburg and his colleagues at the Stanford University History Education Group have developed document-based instructional lessons for uncovering historical events and people. In their model, "facts are mastered by engaging students in historical questions that spark their curiosity and make them passionate about seeking answers." To truly uncover the curriculum, learners must have access to multiple texts and stories, for as the Stanford University historians argue, "It is this rich diet, not the thin gruel of textbooks, that our students need most" (Wineburg, Martin, & Monte-Sano, 2013, p. xii). The goal is for students and teachers alike to think historically and "see patterns, make sense of contradictions, and formulate reasoned interpretations" (Wineburg, Martin, & Monte-Sano, 2013, p. ix).

EXPANDING LEARNING WITH CONTRASTING CONTENT

An approach called "contrasting content" offers a framework for weaving hidden histories and untold stories into standards-based curriculums (Maloy & LaRoche, 2015). Contrasting content emerges when students and teachers juxtapose information presented in frameworks and textbooks with experiences and topics traditionally left untold in the curriculum. The premise of contrasting content is that "history looked at under the surface, in the streets and on the farms, in GI barracks and trailer camps, in factories and offices, tells a different story" (Zinn & Arnove, 2009, p. 24). In the words of a student teacher from one of our teaching methods courses, contrasting content "includes providing competing narratives, untold stories, and ideas that may not be widely known with respect to a topic."

To integrate hidden histories and untold stories, students and teachers focus on three aspects of curriculum exploration:

(1) Individuals and groups whose experiences are omitted when teaching a curriculum standard; for example, the histories of women, people of

color, workers, and LGBTQ individuals and groups during time periods in history as well as contemporary society.

(2) Concepts and terms related to, but left unexplored, when teaching a curriculum standard. A standard about federalism, separation of powers, and the system of checks and balances in American government, for example, might include material about Vermont's Citizen Legislature as a case where politicians serve on a part-time rather than a full-time basis. Furthermore, examining the roles of corporate money and full-time lobbyists in financing bills and influencing elections could generate a contrast between the organizational structures of governmental systems described in textbooks and current realities of contemporary American politics.

(3) Topics and issues revealing citizen activism that are often not discussed when teaching a curriculum standard. For example, an economics standard on the role of buyers and sellers in determining prices might include material on present-day consumer boycotts as well as the story of Cesar Chavez, Dolores Huerta, and the United Farmworkers grape boycott as well as other occasions of strikes and labor unrest in American history. Similarly, a standard on the Bill of Rights could include current struggles for transgender rights at state and national levels.

ENLARGING STUDENT UNDERSTANDINGS

The Transportation Revolution and *Luddites and the Industrial Revolution*, pages on *resourcesforhistoryteachers* wiki, show ways to make hidden histories and untold stories part of learning standards that do not mention diverse history topics within the text of the standard.

Page Example: The Transportation Revolution

> Visit *The Transportation Revolution* page at
> https://resourcesforhistoryteachers.wikispaces.com/USI.27

The Transportation Revolution is a term used to describe the dramatic infrastructure changes occurring in the United States in the early years of the nineteenth century. In 1800, Americans relied on horse-drawn wagons to transport goods over poorly maintained roads, a mode of transportation that took considerable time and manpower. It took, for instance, four days to move goods from New York City to Boston or Albany or Washington, D.C., a week to get to Pittsburgh, and twenty-eight days to get to Detroit. By 1816, the cost of shipping a ton of goods thirty miles overland in the United States was the same as shipping that same ton across the Atlantic Ocean to England. As a result, eastern and western markets within the nation's growing market economy remained largely disconnected from one another.

Development of canals, roads, bridges, turnpikes, steamboats, and railroads dramatically changed the economy. These technological and mechanical innovations made the movement of goods and people significantly easier and much less expensive, ushering in an "Era of Good Feelings" during the presidency of James Monroe. To cover and discover this topic, contributors to the *Transportation Revolution* page on *resourcesforhistoryteachers* posted multiple interactive multimodal resources:

- A description of the National Road, the nation's first federally funded highway, from a Federal Highway Administration website;
- a graph comparing costs in 1800 and 1850 for transportation by horse-drawn wagons, railroads, canal boats, and steamboats;
- a map of major canals built in the Northeastern United States during the first half of the nineteenth century;
- a video on the Transportation Revolution;
- an 1839 painting by W. H. Bartlett of a lockport on the Erie Canal;
- a link to an independent researcher's site containing dozens of primary source images of the building of the Erie Canal.

Adding contrasting content/hidden histories/untold stories to this standard begins by asking who built the roads, canals, and railroads; who helped transport the goods; and how people's lives were impacted by social and economic change of the time. The Chesapeake and Ohio National Park website has the histories of African Americans who worked the canal boats, tended the mules, and loaded and unloaded cargo, but were banned from captaining vessels. That site also describes how C&O canal was a route on the Underground Railroad for southern slaves seeking freedom.

Further exploring the experiences of African Americans, Thomas C. Buchanan (2004, p. 79) in his book *Black Life on the Mississippi* notes how the division of labor on steamboats reflected long-standing hierarchies of social and economic discrimination: "The disparity in power between the mostly native white officers and the motley mix of European immigrants, African Americans, and native whites in the deck crews reproduced enduring conflicts." These stories expand how students understand who benefited and who did not from the transportation revolution's expanding commercial economy.

There are other hidden history stories connected to railroad and the Transportation Revolution. "Tears, Trains and Triumphs," a site from the Railroad

Museum of Pennsylvania explores the historical legacy of African Americans in the building of early railroads. Black slaves were used to construct portions of the Baltimore and Ohio railroad in Maryland in the 1830s while by 1850 two-thirds of North Carolina's railroad workers were African Americans, serving as firemen, brakemen, steamfitters, and mechanics, but not engineers as that was prohibited by state law. After the Civil War, the building of the Transcontinental Railroad includes multiple diverse history stories about Chinese railway workers, Native Americans, women, and working-class groups whose lives and cultures were impacted by changing patterns of migration and transportation.

Page Example: The Luddites and the Industrial Revolution

Visit the *Luddites and the Industrial Revolution* page at https://resourcesforhistoryteachers.wikispaces.com/WHII.6

As broad statements about history, curriculum standards do not reference all groups or events that may relate to that standard. Students and teachers create contrasting content by finding and adding stories of who and/or what has been hidden or untold. A world history standard on the social and economic impact of the early Industrial Revolution is an illustration of this strategy in action incorporating the experiences of workers and working classes in the Luddite Rebellion of 1811–1813.

Luddites were skilled workers who protested widespread unemployment and economic hard times by smashing machines (called frame-breaking) and even setting on fire some factories in midlands England between 1811 and 1816. The term "Luddite" took hold in the popular imagination at the time, and it has lasted in the English language. In modern-day usage, the term has a strongly disparaging connotation: a Luddite is a technophobe who thoughtlessly and stubbornly opposes technological progress and change.

But, as historian Kevin Binfield (2015, p. 3) has noted after analyzing letters, songs, poems, and other writings by these protesting workers, Luddites were not mindless rejecters of technology. They "opposed the use of machines whose purposes was to reduce production costs," thus taking jobs away from workers. Weavers, for example, "sought to eliminate the steam-powered looms that were driving down wages in the cotton trade." Indeed, noted Binfield (2015, p. xiii), Luddite activity "formed only part of a continuum of popular protest against new technology in the Industrial Revolution."

There was no single movement, but a series of overlapping protests that began long before 1811 and continued throughout the early nineteenth century. In these cases, facing a technological replacement of their skilled labor, workers "turned to wrecking the offensive machines to preserve their jobs and trades" (Binfield, 2015, p. 4).

Multiple resources for studying the Luddites on *resourcesforhistoryteachers* include:

- An 1812 drawing of two frame-breakers smashing a loom from the Wikimedia Commons website;
- a brief historical overview of the Luddites from the UK National Archives;
- an article entitled "What the Luddites Really Fought Against" by Richard Conniff from *Smithsonian Magazine* (March, 2011);
- primary source material including a Luddite oath, letters written to unemployed knitters, and an excerpt from Charlotte Bronte's 1849 novel, *Shirley, A Tale*.

Additional research can add to these resources and deepen the analysis of the Luddites protests as well as other occasions when workers or peasants rebelled against oppressive conditions and arbitrary authorities.

TEACHING DIVERSE HISTORIES

Every state or local curriculum framework has some standards organized around diverse history topics. In U.S. history are standards dealing with relations between native peoples and European settlers; women's suffrage; Andrew Jackson's policy of Indian removal and the Trail of Tears; abolitionism; the passage of the Thirteenth, Fourteenth, and Fifteenth Amendments; the *Plessy v. Ferguson* and *Brown v. Board of Education* Supreme Court decisions; and the post-World War II civil rights and women's rights movements. In world history are standards focusing on the "Golden Age" of Islamic civilizations, the trans-Atlantic slave trade and the abolition of slavery within the British Empire, expansion of voting rights around the world, Indian nationalism and the nonviolence resistance of Gandhi, the causes and consequences of the Holocaust, and Nelson Mandela and the fall of apartheid in South Africa.

Even when standards have a multicultural focus, teachers and students do not always widely explore the experiences of diverse individuals and groups within and across time periods. Here are two examples, the Civil Rights Movement and the historical experiences of women in the workforce.

To date, reported researchers from the Southern Poverty Law Center's Teaching Tolerance Project (2012, p. 4), most state curriculum frameworks have "routinely ignored or over-simplified the struggles of African Americans for civil rights that took place in the 1950s and 1960s." Students learn mainly about the efforts of "two heroic figures—Martin Luther King and Rosa Parks—and the four words 'I have a dream.' " Grading the states on a scale of 0 to 100 as to how the principal actors of major events in civil rights history are chronicled, no state received a score above 70 percent while the average grade was an F.

According to the Southern Poverty Law Center, part of the issue is that most state history standards share two basic characteristics. First, they broadly identify the historical content that students are expected to learn, focusing mainly on well-known people and events. Lesser known individual and events do not make the narrative. Second, most state standards, organized using Benjamin Bloom's lower order to higher order thinking skills framework, emphasize remembering historical information rather than critical analysis and application of ideas. As a result, students learn selected names and dates, but not the underlying dynamics of slavery and segregation in American society (Southern Poverty Law Center Teaching Tolerance Project, 2014).

In the case of African American civil rights history, most states have failed to connect the "civil rights movement to other social movements" by not requiring "coverage across grade levels," by not including "movement-related instruction in the civics curriculum," and by not connecting civil rights history to current events (Southern Poverty Law Center's Teaching Tolerance Project, 2012, p. 7).

In a post on the Zinn Education Project's "If We Only Knew Our History" website, teacher Adam Sanchez (2016) makes a similar point about the inadequacies of civil rights history. Noting that textbooks routinely stop discussing civil rights with the passage of the 1965 Voting Rights Act and the assassination of Martin Luther King, Jr., Sanchez proposes educators uncover "the Long Civil Rights Movement" that stretches from the 1930s to the 1970s and beyond to today. In every decade, there are hidden histories and untold stories to tell, including urban rebellions, the Black Power Movement, the Black Panther Party, the Memphis Sanitation Workers Strike, the Orangeburg Massacre, the Attica Prison Uprising, and the Boston School Busing Crisis.

When teaching about civil rights of African American or any other diverse history group, teachers, in addressing the required standards, must also integrate contrasting content resources that expand how elementary, middle, and high school students understand people's experiences.

Page Example: The Civil Rights Movement

Visit *The Civil Rights Movement* page at https://resourcesforhistory-teachers.wikispaces.com/USII.25

A civil rights movement page on *resourcesforhistoryteachers* has primary source, film and video, text resources, and biography materials for each of the major topics and leaders listed in the Massachusetts curriculum framework. In addition, the page has the following contrasting content/hidden history/ untold story resources:

- Historical Biography page for Bayard Rustin, the gay civil rights activist who was the core organizer of the 1963 March on Washington.
- Links to a page on the Latino Civil Rights Movement with material on the 1947 *Mendez v. Westminster* court case and the 1965–1970 Delano Grape Strike and Boycott.
- Links to information about Claudette Colvin and other African American women who refused to give up seats and move back in Montgomery Alabama city buses in the months before Rosa Parks' legendary protest. The actions of these women lead to the 1956 *Browder v. Gayle* U.S. district court case that ruled segregation on buses unconstitutional.
- References to Shirley Chisholm's achievements in politics as an African American woman, including being the first black woman elected to Congress in 1968, a founding member of the Congressional Black Caucus, and the first African American presidential candidate in 1972.
- A link to an influential literature page about the young adult novel, *The Watsons Go to Birmingham—1963* by Christopher Paul Curtis, that tells the story of ten-year-old Kenny and his family from Michigan who journey to the American South in 1963 during a time of racial violence against African Americans. The 16th Street Baptist Church Bombing is a centerpiece of the novel.

Many other histories and stories are available to be added; that is how the purpose of a wiki, where multiple contributors continue expanding page content to inform a community of interested readers and learners, achieves its possibilities for information access.

Page Examples: Lowell Mill Girls; Women in World War I; and Women in World War II

Visit *Lowell Mill Girls* page at
https://resourcesforhistoryteachers.wikispaces.com/Lowell+Mill+Girls
Visit *Women in World War I* page at
https://resourcesforhistoryteachers.wikispaces.com/Women+in+World+War+I

Visit *Women in World War II* at
https://resourcesforhistoryteachers.wikispaces.com/Women+in+World+
War+II

Linking a series of wiki pages based on the experiences of a social group
serves to uncover hidden histories and untold stories across different time
periods and curriculum standards. The idea for this approach comes from an
online National Women's History Museum (NWHM) exhibit, "A History
of Women in Industry" that focuses on women's participation in the paid
labor force during three time periods—Industrial Revolution (1800–1860);
Progressive Era (1880–1900); and Depression/World War I (1930–1945).
The exhibit's theme is how "women's varied experiences in the labor force
and in labor organizations have tended to challenge dominant definitions
of femininity" at different periods in history (National Women's History
Museum, 2007).

Pages on *resourcesforhistoryteachers* are linked together to create a
multitime period approach to women's roles as workers: *Lowell Mill Girls,
Women in World War I*, and *Women in World II*. In presenting information
about women's roles, each page features key topics, including the first union
of working women and the Lowell Mill Girls strikes of 1834 and 1836; wom-
en's work in factories as well as with the Red Cross, the Patriotic League, and
the Young Women's Christian Association (YWCA) during World War I;
and the experiences of Rosie the Riveter and other women workers in World
War II.

Each page also uncovers hidden histories and untold stories, including new
research suggesting that inspiration for Dickens' Christmas Carol may have
come from his visit to the Lowell Mills in 1842; the connections that formed
between women's labor activism and other social reform movements such
as suffrage and the abolition of slavery; the Munitionettes (English women
armory workers during World War I); the Fly Girls (World War II women
pilots); and Top Secret Rosies (women mathematicians who did ballistics
research, including calculating weapons trajectories for soldiers and pilots
during World War II).

Students and teachers can further expand history and humanities topics by
researching the leadership of women, contrasting their experiences in differ-
ent parts of the country and in wartime and peacetime in U.S. history. Clara
Barton's singular vision and forceful presence as a founder of the American
Red Cross is a unique story of one woman shaping history during the Civil
War and throughout time; women's work experiences during World War

I and World War II set the course for changing expectations of women's roles after the wars.

Wiki pages, connected around the experiences of different societal groups, like those for the Civil Rights Movement and women in the workforce, offer ways to study people and events thematically. Students and teachers can move between different time periods, comparing and contrasting people's experiences. New information is easily added to existing pages, and additional pages can be built to extend the stream of information, in each case uncovering further histories and stories that make the curriculum more inclusive and more meaningful for students.

INTEGRATING LGBTQ EXPERIENCES

A focus on LGBTQ (Lesbian, Gay, Bisexual, Transgender, and Queer) people and history is another way to use wikis to integrate hidden histories and untold stories into curriculum. LGBTQ history has been largely excluded from curriculum standards and mainstream textbooks, but as historian Michael Bronski (2011, p. xii) stated, the "contributions of people who we may now identify as lesbian, gay, bisexual, or transgender are integral and central to how we conceptualize our national history." LGBTQ people must not be studied apart from the "broader sweep and breadth of American history."

In 2011, a groundbreaking law, California's FAIR (Fair, Accurate, Inclusive, Respectful) Education Act, mandated the inclusion of lesbian, gay, bisexual, and transgender people in public school history classes, stating that students and teachers must study:

> the role and contributions of both men and women, Native Americans, African Americans, Mexican **Americans**, Asian **Americans**, Pacific Islanders, **European Americans, lesbian, gay, bisexual, and transgender Americans, persons with disabilities**, and members of other ethnic **and cultural** groups, to the economic, political, and social development of California and the United States of America, with particular emphasis on portraying the role of these groups in contemporary society (California Department of Education, 2015: bold print added in the original source).

Hailed as a milestone in making history education more inclusive, the FAIR Act has been implemented slowly by schools in the state, in part because of opposition from antigay rights groups, and in part because it is not clear how to develop curriculum around topics of gender and sexuality at the different K–12 grade levels.

To achieve full implementation of the FAIR Education Act, a committee of historians and educators has proposed a "transformational approach," organized around a "convergence of multiple stories" (Romesburg, Rupp, & Donahue, 2014). In their view, students and teachers study LGBT families in Grade 2, the roles of gender and sexuality in California's history in Grade 4, an exploration of colonial America's gender-related laws and social practices in Grade 5, changes in gender and sexuality roles and norms during nineteenth-century urbanization and industrialization in Grade 8, and twentieth century's rise of the gay civil rights movement in the context of discrimination and persecution of sexual and gender minorities in Grade 11.

In teaching LGBTQ history, the authors of the report, "Making the Framework FAIR," urge educators to adopt the lessons learned from teaching about the experiences of other historically oppressed groups. They note "the best teaching on the histories of people of color has evolved from an additive 'race heroes' model to the understanding of race as a lens of historical analysis" (Romesburg, Rupp, & Donahue, 2014, p. 6). The actions of LGBTQ individuals and groups must be understood in the larger political, economic, and social context of the times in which they lived. LGBTQ curriculum should not present sexuality as a "relevant characteristic only of LGBT people, it limits our understanding of identity and of the ways sexuality operates at levels from the individual to the transnational" (Romesburg, Rupp, & Donahue, 2014, p. 5).

To integrate the hidden histories and untold stories of LGBTQ experience into school or classroom wikis, students and teachers may follow one of these strategies: (1) focusing on individuals; (2) examining dramatic events; and (3) integrating LGBTQ resources on learning standard pages.

Page Example: Alan Turing

Visit *Alan Turing* page:
https://resourcesforhistoryteachers.wikispaces.com/Alan+Turing

---

Focusing on individuals create opportunities to contextualize personal experience within larger historical contexts while expanding existing curriculum frameworks. For example, a wiki page describing mathematician and computer scientist Alan Turing can expand a curriculum standard about the work of twentieth century-scientists, notably Albert Einstein, J. Robert Oppenheimer, Jonas Salk, James Watson, and Francis Crick and the breakthrough work they did that changed scientific paradigms and understandings. Turing's accomplishments, in conjunction with others, breaking the World War II enigma code, developing the Universal Turing Machine (a forerunner to the modern computer), and starting the field of artificial intelligence, can be understood in the context of his closeted life as a gay man and his death by suicide in 1954 following a humiliating indecency conviction by the very government his research helped to save.

Page Examples: Integrating LGBTQ Histories

Visit *The Stonewall Uprising* page at https://resourcesforhistoryteachers.wikispaces.com/The+Stone wall+Uprising

A second integration strategy involves examining dramatic historical events, for as Elizabeth Gartley (2015) noted in a column for the Gay, Lesbian, Bisexual, and Transgender Round Table of the American Library Association, "some of the most significant moments in LGBT history are already common topics of study in U.S. History and World History classrooms, but LGBT experiences and lives have been erased from the history books."

A page on *resourcesforhistoryteachers* for the Stonewall Uprising, an event that propelled the modern LGBTQ rights movement, features primary source materials as well as multimedia resources for learning about the event at the Stonewall Inn in SoHo, New York City and its lasting impacts on the gay rights movement. Connected pages can then be constructed about other LGBTQ topics such as shifting gender roles in the 1920s, changing military policies about gay soldiers, the Lavender Scare, AIDS, and legal battles over same-sex marriage—just to name some pivotal twentieth-century history topics (Eaklor, 2011).

Page Examples: Selected Standards Pages

https://resourcesforhistoryteachers.wikispaces.com/WHI.7
https://resourcesforhistoryteachers.wikispaces.com/USI.9
https://resourcesforhistoryteachers.wikispaces.com/Bayard+Rustin
https://resourcesforhistoryteachers.wikispaces.com/USI.38
https://resourcesforhistoryteachers.wikispaces.com/WHII.26

A third strategy involves including LGBTQ topics in curriculum learning standard pages. Marking resources with a rainbow flag, contributors to *resourcesforhistoryteachers* have added LGBTQ history to many different standards, including the role of civil unions for male couples as part of a world history standard about economic, social, and political developments in medieval Europe; an infographic on LGBTQ rights around the world on a U.S. history standard about the passage of the Bill of Rights; a biography page introducing Bayard Rustin added to an AP U.S. standard on the 1960s; material on how Walt Whitman's Civil War experiences affected his writing included in a U.S. standard on the Civil War; and the history of Nazi persecution of homosexuals within a standard on the Holocaust.

Making LGBTQ experience part of pages devoted to specific world and U.S. history curriculum standards serves to reinforce the idea that students and teachers need to explore the interconnected experiences of people during different time periods as essential elements of history and humanities learning. Teaching one group's history separate and disconnected from the rest of society is a limited approach to curriculum for it leaves peoples' experiences isolated from one another. Integrating LGBTQ history to the teaching of curriculum standards—just as integrating women's history, African American history, Native American history or the history of any other dispossessed group—serves to widen how students and teachers alike view society and understand human experience.

The three types of LGBTQ wiki pages discussed in this section—as well as pages that explore the histories of people of color, women, and working-class individuals and groups—enable teachers and students to uncover neglected events and untold stories from the past. In so doing, they expand the curriculum multiculturally and multimodally, pushing teaching and learning beyond the focus of mainstream textbooks and state curriculum frameworks. Addressing hidden histories also opens explorations of dramatic events, notable individuals and influential works of literature, the basis for the next two chapters in this book.

Chapter 5

Exploring Dramatic Events and Special Topics

The 1950s Lavender Scare was the U.S. federal government's persecution of gay and lesbian civil servants during the height of the McCarthy era in American politics. Though not mentioned in most curriculum frameworks or history textbooks, the dismissal of thousands of government employees based on their alleged sexual orientation was a dramatic event at the time. Observed historian David K. Johnson (2004, pp. 2, 4), "Many politicians, journalists, and citizens thought that homosexuals posed more of a threat to national security than Communists." More than just a part of the decade's Red Scare, Johnson argues these "purges predicated McCarthy, became institutionalized within the federal loyalty/security system, and continued to be standard government policy until the 1970s."

The story of Lavender Scare introduces how teacher- and student-made wikis can be used to explore dramatic events and special topics as part of the history and humanities curriculum. Dramatic events are pivotal moments in history; focal points for classroom study. Some dramatic events are iconic, found in most textbooks, curriculum frameworks, and school district lesson plans (the Lewis & Clark Expedition, the Irish Potato Famine, the Cuban Missile Crisis); others like the Lavender Scare are important historical developments that are not widely discussed in schools. Special topics are issues that concern society (climate change and global warming, world hunger, the role of the Electoral College in American elections); they are the subject of debates and choices made by people at different times for different reasons.

This chapter illustrates how building Dramatic Event and Special Topic pages in teacher- and student-made wikis provide a basis for social, economic, and political analysis of past and present. Standards-based wiki pages described in chapter 1 facilitate a wide-angle view of history and humanities curriculum; Dramatic Event and Special Topic pages narrow the view to how people experience history-shaping turning points. The chapter considers the "what to teach" and "coverage vs. depth" dilemmas facing teachers and students before discussing ways to build Dramatic Event and Special Topic wiki pages by Opening up the Textbook (OUT), examining events thematically, and investigating issues through inquiry-based learning.

THE "WHAT TO TEACH" QUESTION

In history and humanities classes, students and teachers confront an ever-present question of how to cover the content in the standards and the textbook. At every grade level, far more historical material exists to learn than time to introduce, connect, and study it. The result is choices are made about what topics to examine in depth, to mention only briefly, and to not discuss at all. As historian William H. McNeill (1985) observed more than three decades ago,

> The varieties of history are enormous; facts and probabilities about the past are far too numerous for anyone to comprehend them all. Every sort of human group has its own history; so do ideas, institutions, techniques, areas, civilizations, and humanity at large. How to begin? Where to start? How bring some sort of order to the enormous variety of things known and believed about the past?

History and humanities curriculum frameworks complicate the "what to teach" process with broadly framed standards that encompass large time periods and list many important events. The Massachusetts standard World History I.7 asks students and teachers to be able to "describe the major economic, social and political development in medieval Europe," a sweep of 1,000 years of history. The standard's subparts include the growing influence of Christianity and the Catholic Church; the differing orders of medieval society; the development of feudalism; the development of private property; the initial emergence of a modern economy; the growth of banking, commerce, towns, and a merchant class; the economic and social effects of the spread of the Black Death or bubonic plague; and the growth and development of the English and French nations (Massachusetts Department of Education, 2003, p. 52).

Similarly expansive, the Massachusetts U.S. history Standard II.6: *Analyze the causes and course of America's growing role in world affairs from the Civil War to World War I* asks teachers and students to examine Social Darwinism; the purchase of Alaska; the annexation of Hawaii; the Spanish-American War; the Open Door Policy; the Roosevelt Corollary to the Monroe Doctrine; the Panama Canal; Dollar Diplomacy; President Wilson's intervention into Mexico; and the American entry into World War I (Massachusetts Department of Education, 2003, p. 73).

Other states' frameworks similarly list multiple events within learning standards. South Carolina initially frames American foreign policy from the Civil War to World War I with the expectation, "The student will demonstrate an understanding of domestic and foreign developments that contributed to the emergence of the United States as a world power in the twentieth century." The framework writers recommend that students and teachers "summarize United States foreign policies in different regions of the world during the early twentieth century, including the purposes and effects of the Open Door policy with China, the United States role in the Panama Revolution, Theodore Roosevelt's 'big stick diplomacy,' William Taft's 'dollar diplomacy,' Woodrow Wilson's 'moral diplomacy,' and changing worldwide perceptions of the United States" (South Carolina Department of Education, 2012).

South Carolina's curriculum framework offers guidance to teachers by including statements about what is "essential for students to know" and what is "not essential for students to know" within each learning standard. Nevertheless, the "it is essential for students to know" description for the emergence of the United States as a world power at the beginning of the twentieth century is over 500 words long and asks students and teachers to learn about multiple events and developments in different parts of the world (South Carolina Department of Education, 2012).

Beyond the academic content specified in a curriculum standard, there are the complimentary skills of critical thinking, writing, and historical analysis that students are expected to learn. These skills extend across curriculum standards, so that students can apply these reasoning skills to topics ranging from historical events to literary genres. Finding ways for students to think like historians, understand writing as writers do, think sociologically and psychologically about events are challenges facing every teacher at every grade level.

For many teachers, developing essential questions for students to explore is an effective way to answer the "what to teach question." An essential question focuses inquiry and analysis; the question motivates students to use academic information and historical evidence to develop answers. Essential questions mirror how scholars conduct research in history and humanities fields; examining people and events, they start not with conclusions but with questions (Wineburg, Martin, & Monte-Sano, 2013, p. x).

Essential questions direct inquiry learning across the grade levels. As Sam Wineburg and his colleagues noted, an investigation of social impacts of Thomas Edison's inventions can be framed by the core question: "Electricity and women's work: Who really benefitted and when?" (Wineburg, Martin, & Monte-Sano, 2013, p. xi). Similarly, a class studying conflicts between traditionalism and modernism in the United States during first decades of the twentieth century might ask "In what ways is F. Scott Fitzgerald's *Great*

Gatsby an accurate portrayal of the social, economic and cultural trends of the 1920s?" Essential questions can also frame the content of Dramatic Event and Special Topic wiki pages, guiding the development of the pages while providing students and teachers with the resources they need to respond to the questions by analyzing sources and interpretations.

COVERAGE AND DEPTH

While densely packed standards in state curriculum frameworks could easily be the curriculum basis for semester-long college courses, teachers are expected to "cover" each standard's key events in just a few classes before moving on to the next group of historical events. In the rapid flow of information, students can experience confusion and boredom with little lasting learning. Awash in names, dates, facts, and places, they lose sight of larger issues and themes. "In the rush to take 9th graders from Mesopotamia to the French Revolution," remarked one educator, "students did not end up either knowing broad swaths of history or how to do historical inquiry" (Mehta, 2015).

Progressive educators have long sought to shift the prevailing pedagogy of history/humanities education away from teacher-centered presentations of broad information toward focused student-centered activities and inquiries. More than two decades ago, Bruce VanSledright (1997, p. 41) urged teachers to explore fewer topics in greater depth:

> Rather than give shallow coverage to everything within a domain of knowledge, I would stress major principles and generalizations and focus in depth on a few examples chosen either because they were prototypical representations of important principles and generalizations or because they provided a good contrast to the examples that are most familiar to students in the United States.

Reflecting on his remarks more than a decade later, VanSledright (2011, p. 21) sees little change in the dominant pedagogy of content coverage; most public school history teachers define their job as "pressing on the storyline, imploring students to read and consume the textbook, reinforcing those details in class each day, and assessing possession of them at the end of the unit." The reason, according to VanSledright (2011, p. 22), is the widely held "socializing Americanization mission" of history education. Teachers see their role as conveying the story of America to students who are expected to "acquire the narrative and repeat it and its details on command." Lost is "teaching history as an investigative act, as a program of digging into the nation's past in order to understand it more deeply."

On its *World History for All of Us* website, the National Center for History in the Schools (NCHS), housed at the University of California Los Angeles

(UCLA), offers one useful way to address the dilemma of coverage versus depth. NCHS proposes that teachers and students explore history using three different types of curriculum units. "Panorama units" are a large-scale, wide-angle view of big eras in history—the goal being for students to gain a broad overview on developments throughout the world during that era. "Landscape units," while not as broad as panorama units, are a transregional, cross-cultural, or comparative look at what is happening in different places during an historical time period. "Close-up units" narrow the focus to specific developments in specific places through more in-depth study of people and events.

In these approaches, for example, the years 1400–1800 CE could be taught using a panorama unit that focuses on the entire era of global interchanges, a landscape unit that focuses on the biological, social, and cultural consequences of the Columbian Exchange, and/or a close-up unit on Enlightenment thinkers, the Atlantic Slave Trade or the Age of Revolutions. Developing a class wiki, students and teachers could locate resources for panorama and landscape units and connect those resources to local or state curriculum standards. Then, building a foundation for more in-depth study, they can develop dramatic event or special topic pages for close-up explorations of significant events, important developments, and influential individuals and groups.

DRAMATIC EVENT WIKI PAGES

History and humanities classes at every grade level examine significant or milestone events in different historical time periods. Learning about "dramatic moments," students and teachers collectively "delve into the deeper meanings of selected landmark events and explore their wider context in the greater historical narrative" (Symcox, 1991, p. 4). In a dramatic moment approach, textbook readings and teacher presentations provide a chronology of events, setting the context for why an event itself might be considered a "crucial turning-point in history." Then examining primary sources and other sources of historical evidence, students become "aware that choices had to be made by real human beings, that those decisions were the result of specific factors, and that they set in motion a series of historical consequences" (Symcox, 1991, p. 4).

A Dramatic Event wiki page cross-links significant or milestone events to state or local learning standards through a combination of the following resources:

- *Event Summary and Essential Question(s)*. Located at the top of the page, an Event Summary is a short overview of the event. It may also include a link to an online summary provided by a digital textbook or historical organization along with secondary source material about the event. One or two essential questions add an investigatory framework for students and teachers to use as they explore the event and its historical meanings.

- *Primary Sources.* Sources include links to original documents related to the event from historical organizations, museums, government agencies, media outlets, college and university sources, and independent researchers and teachers.
- *Images and Pictures.* Pictures, photographs, and artwork depicting historical events and people are placed throughout the page to expand how readers think about a topic or standard. As much as possible, images and pictures are public domain and freely licensed materials found on Wikimedia Commons and other image repositories.
- *Multimedia resources.* Video or audio materials from YouTube, Smithsonian, Library of Congress and other sources provide multimodal listening and viewing experiences for teachers and students.
- *Multicultural/Women's/LGBTQ history resources.* Links to online resources reveal hidden histories and untold stories of people and events.
- *Lesson Plans and Other Teaching and Learning Resources.* Materials for inquiry-based learning experiences include instructional plans for teachers and interactive websites, serious learning games, and other hands-on learning opportunities for students.

"Annexation of Hawaii" and "Building the Panama Canal"—two American foreign policy events between the Civil War and World War I—are examples of Dramatic Event wiki pages. Hawaiian annexation and the Panama Canal construction reveal not only the dynamics of imperialism of the time but also the roles of American business interests and the responses by native peoples to American expansionism. The resources on each page, blended together, offer a wide-angle view of historical events for classroom discussion and analysis.

Page Example: Annexation of Hawaii

Visit the *Annexation of Hawaii* page:
https://resourcesforhistoryteachers.wikispaces.com/Annexation+
of+Hawaii

- *Event Summary and Essential Question*: *Annexation of Hawaii* from Digital History, a site from the University of Houston that includes an online textbook with short overviews of events in American history listed by historical era. The page's Essential Question is "How Did Imperialism Affect America's Influence throughout Asia and the Pacific Region?"

* *Images*: Three photographs frame the event, "Raising American Flag at 'Iolani Palace, Honolulu, Hawaii, August 12, 1898; portrait of "Queen Liliuokalani"; and a picture of "Sanford Ballard Dole, first governor after American annexation." The photos record a key moment and identify two important historical figures in the history of the islands.

* *Primary Sources*: "Joint Resolution to Provide for Annexing the Hawaiian Islands to the United States, December 6, 1898," and "Letter from Queen Liliuokalani Protesting U.S. Assertion of Ownership of Hawaii, December 19, 1898." These sources from the National Archives present the perspectives of American policymakers and native leaders.

* *Multicultural History*: A biography of Queen Liliuokalani from the National Women's History Museum and links the origins of the Dole Food Company and the Pineapple Trade. The biography integrates women's history into the event while the Dole Food Company materials reveal the importance of the pineapple trade to guiding American actions at the time.

* *Lesson Plans and Teaching Ideas*: "America Becomes a Pacific Nation: Hawaiian Annexation" from Portland State University has engaging lessons focusing not only on Hawaii but also on American policies in the Pacific region.

Page Example: Building the Panama Canal

Visit the *Building the Panama Canal* page:
https://resourcesforhistoryteachers.wikispaces.com/Panama+Canal

* *Event Summary and Essential Question*: "Building the Panama Canal, 1903–1914" from the Office of the Historian, U.S. Department of State, a site that features short descriptions of American foreign policy events throughout history, is one excellent summary. "Theodore Roosevelt and the Panama Canal" from PBS American Experience offers a video introduction to the building of the canal. The page's Essential Question is "What Methods Did the U.S. Use to Establish and Expand Its Empire?"

* *Visual Images*: Two photographs can be used to frame the page, a "Modern-Day View of the Canal Looking West, 2002" from NASA satellite image and the "Panama Canal under Construction, 1907" from the Library of Congress. An image of a man spraying kerosene oil to kill mosquitoes introduces the topic of malaria, an ancient disease that still threatens people in the world today.

- **Primary Sources**: "Panama Canal Proposal," 1881, a letter by Ulysses S. Grant from Gilder Lehrman Institute of American History; "Roosevelt's Message to Congress," December 17, 1906 from PBS American Experience; and "The Story of the Panama Canal," 1927, a film from the Roosevelt Film Library made available online by the Library of Congress offer insights into the perspectives of American leaders who advocated for the canal.
- **Multimedia Resources**: "Make the Dirt Fly!" an online exhibit from the Smithsonian and "The Panama Canal," a YouTube-posted video segment from Seven Wonders of the World from the BBC offer multimodal learning experiences in the forms of an interactive website and a short video segment.
- **Multicultural History**: "Panama Canal and Malaria" from the Centers for Disease Control and Prevention; "Yellow Fever and Malaria in the Canal" from PBS American Experience; and "Mosquitoes, Malaria and the Panama Canal," an excerpt from David McCullough's book *The Path between the Seas* present background on one of the hidden history/untold stories of the canal.
- **Lesson Plans and Teaching Ideas**: "The Question of an American Empire" from EDSITEment, National Endowment for the Humanities explores the Panama Canal in the larger context of American expansion at the time.

OPENING UP THE TEXTBOOK

Opening Up the Textbook (OUT), a teaching strategy from the Stanford History Education Group and the National History Education Clearinghouse, presents another way to use textbooks together with the learning resources collected on Dramatic Event wiki pages to address the "what the teach" dilemma. In this approach, the textbook becomes a source to be questioned and analyzed rather than an account to be remembered while wiki pages are used to expand the types of information that students can access about an event (Wineburg, 2007).

To conduct an Opening Up the Textbook activity, a teacher "juxtaposes a short excerpt from the course textbook" with other historically relevant materials, often primary sources (National History Education Clearinghouse, n.d.). Students examine the information, compare and contrast it with textbook accounts, and use the materials to formulate thoughtful questions and construct more in-depth and detailed explanations for what happened and why. In so doing, the textbook is expanded by the inclusion of multiple voices, diverse perspectives, and surprising information—all intended to promote new insights among students.

The story of Rosa Parks' role in the Montgomery Bus Boycott is a memorable example of how an Opening Up the Textbook (OUT) activity can generate new learning for students and teachers. For many years, textbooks said "Rosa was Tired," a myth in which she refused to give up her seat at the front of the bus simply because she was exhausted from a long day of work as a seamstress (Kohl, 1991).

In fact, Rosa Parks was a lifelong political activist whose participation in the Civil Rights movement began when she was a young woman (Theoharis, 2014). Her protest against racial segregation in public transportation on December 1, 1955, was not the first time that she had been put off a city bus for not following directions of the driver. But when she boarded the bus on that day, unaware that the driver was someone she avoided riding with, she was arrested for refusing his request to move from her seat. What looked to be a spontaneous action that launched the 381-day Montgomery Bus Boycott, brought the Reverend Dr. Martin Luther King, Jr. to the forefront of American attention and ignited the Civil Rights Movement was the result of intentional civil disobedience that the NAACP had been preparing to do for months.

In an Opening Up the Textbook lesson from *Historical Thinking Matters* (2008), a website from the Roy Rosenzweig Center for History and New Media at George Mason University, students read a textbook account and watch a YouTube video about the Montgomery Bus Boycott to frame the historical context. Next they analyze primary source materials that include Jo Ann Robinson's letter to the Mayor of Montgomery asking for fair treatment on the buses, Reverend Ralph Abernathy's oral account of the first meeting of the Montgomery Improvement Association, and an interview with an unnamed African American maid describing the origins of the bus boycott movement. Using textbook excerpt, the video, and the primary source materials, students compose their own answers to the essential question, "Why did the boycott of Montgomery's buses succeed?"

The primary source and multimedia materials that the Historical Thinking Matters project provided for the Rosa Parks lesson are the types of resources that can be assembled on a wiki page to create Opening Up the Textbook activities for different history and humanities topics. In many cases, while newer textbooks may have current historical information, they do not have enough of that information to provide an extraordinary learning experience for students.

Sometimes textbooks mention historical occurrences mainly in passing. Unlike the "Rosa Was Tired" myth that needed to be debunked, the goal in these cases is to expand the textbook by taking a historically accurate piece of information and exploring it more deeply across multiple time periods. Here is an example of expanding the textbook using a wiki page from *resourcesforhistoryteachers* on the experiences of African American Civil War soldiers.

Page Example: African American Civil War Soldiers

> Visit the *African American Civil War Soldiers* page:
> https://resourcesforhistoryteachers.wikispaces.com/USI.39

Historians estimate nearly 180,000 blacks fought in the Union army; another 9,000 served as sailors in the Union navy (Freeman, Schamel, & West, 1992). By war's end, African Americans made up fully 10 percent of all Union forces. From an expanding the textbook perspective, students and teachers can begin with the experiences of the 54th Massachusetts Volunteer Regiment, one of the Union army's first all-black infantry units.

From that starting point, the *resourcesforhistoryteachers* wiki has links to multiple online resources informing the experiences of African American Civil War soldiers: "The Fight for Equal Rights: Black Soldiers in the Civil War," a lesson plan with primary documents from the National Archives; an overview of African American soldiers from the Library of Congress; and a black soldiers' timeline from the website of the PBS film, "The Time of the Lincolns." Then there are African Americans who served in the Union navy; current estimates now suggest that 20 percent of the navy's enlisted force were of African descent. The National Archives has a three-part series of background material called "Black Men in Navy Blue."

The stories of black soldiers create the opportunity to explore the wider experiences of African Americans during the Civil War. Students and teachers can read and discuss Frederick Douglass' impassioned call for black participation in the war, "Men of Color: To Arms! To Arms!" They can evaluate the historical accuracy of the Hollywood movie, *Glory,* which was based on the actions of the 54th Massachusetts troops at the Battle of Fort Wagner in 1863. The wartime actions of enslaved Africans are another topic for classroom study, including those who were forced to support the Confederate war effort and those who successfully escaped bondage. As a further extension, primary sources related to the efforts of black abolitionists can be analyzed.

Students and teachers can then examine the contributions of African Americans soldiers during other wars in American history—the First Rhode Island Regiment during the Revolutionary War; the 10th Cavalry Regiment or Buffalo Soldiers; the 92nd and 93rd Divisions and Harlem Hellfighters during World War I; the Tuskegee Airmen and the Triple Nickels during World War II; President Truman's milestone 1948 Executive Order 9981 to desegregate the military; and experiences of black soldiers in the Korean, Vietnam, and Gulf wars.

EXAMINING EVENTS THEMATICALLY

Whether to teach academic content chronologically or thematically is an ongoing debate among history and humanities educators. Historical chronology, notes teacher Sarah Cooper (2015), gives students and teachers an easy-to-understand structure where *"this* leads to *this* leads to *this,* one after the other." But embedded within the ongoing flow of events are patterns of human experience that remain invisible to students unless brought up by identifying themes and continually connecting people and events to those themes throughout the school year.

Many teachers integrate themes into their teaching. History, noted Diana Laufenberg (2011), "is a series of events and causal relationships, stories, tragedies and successes that when strung together weave narrative of people and places." An overemphasis on historical chronology amounts to giving students "pieces of paper (facts) with no real understanding of how to connect or make meaning." To avoid those pitfalls of chronology, Laufenberg recommends creating themes and then "layer theme over previous themes and discuss connections and patterns and flow and trends that exist."

At the same time, there are multiple challenges to be faced when seeking to connect events thematically. Students and teachers alike need resources that enable them to investigate events and interconnections. Most textbooks explore events within a time period rather than moving back and forth throughout history to discover what preceded and succeeded them. Studies of revolutions, empires, and migrations abound, but those scholarly books may not be easily accessible for classroom use.

Teacher- and student-made wikis can be used to explore events that happened at different times and in different places in history—many of which are not regularly studied thematically as interconnected happenings. Themes might include revolutions, war and conquest, the rise and fall of empires, migrations, movements of people and goods, impacts of technological change, struggles for freedom and resistance to oppression, political change, and many more.

Examining events thematically and comparing their similarities and differences reduces the isolation of studying single situations apart from wider historical patterns and developments. Plagues, pandemics, and disease throughout history offer an example of how wikis can be used to provide a

framework for comparative study of dramatic events impacting human societies, beginning with the 1918 Influenza Pandemic.

Page Example: 1918 Influenza Pandemic

> Visit the *1918 Influenza Pandemic* page:
> https://resourcesforhistoryteachers.wikispaces.com/The+1918+
> Influenza+Pandemc

While disease is a topic in some learning standards and absent from others,
the "history of humanity's encounters with infectious diseases" has resulted
in "far reaching consequences," declared historian William H. McNeill (1998,
p. 21). Smallpox, typhus, cholera, AIDS, and deadly flu viruses have transformed interactions among people, particularly the populations who had not
developed immunities to infection.

The national Advanced Placement (AP) World History Framework references the impacts of infectious diseases in several of its Key Concepts. The
Massachusetts curriculum framework includes the Bubonic Plague (or Black
Death) as part of a standard on the Middle Ages and includes the HIV/AIDS
epidemic as a twentieth-century history standard. But in Massachusetts, as
in other state frameworks, there is no mention of other history-changing
pandemics—the sixth-century Justinian plague that killed 100 million people,
half the population of Europe at the time; the seventeenth-century smallpox,
measles, and influenza epidemics among Native Americans after the arrival
of European settlers; the Pandemic of 1894; or the 1918 Influenza Pandemic
that caused some fifty million deaths worldwide.

Building a dramatic event page for the 1918 Influenza Pandemic and then
cross-linking that page to other pages dealing with plagues and pathogens is
a wiki-based way for students and teachers to engage in comparative explorations of the impacts of disease throughout history. The *1918 Influenza Pandemic* page has links to summaries of the event, primary sources, multimedia
materials, and instructional lesson plans along with cross-links to pages
dealing with HIV/AIDS, Malaria, the Bubonic Plague, the debate over Jef-
frey Amherst and the Smallpox Blankets in colonial Massachusetts, and the
Plague of Justinian in 541–542. All these pages can be continually updated
as researchers locate new evidence for how diseases happen and are spread.

Wikis allow teachers and students to explore people and events thematically by cross-linking pages in one online location. The movements of people
through migration, immigration, and forced relocation can include pages

on the Peopling of the Americas; the Atlantic Slave Trade; the Irish Potato Famine; Chinese immigration to the United States and the transcontinental railroad; the California and Alaska Gold Rushes; the Depression-era Dust Bowl and John Steinbeck's novel, *The Grapes of Wrath*; and modern-day experiences of refugees.

Page Example: Youth Activism in U.S. History

Visit *Youth Activism in U.S. History* page:
http://resourcesforhistoryteachers.wikispaces.com/Youth+Activism+in+U.+S.+History

Thematic wiki pages enable teachers and students to examine trends across decades or centuries. A page on youth activism in U.S. history can feature, upon other topics, Sacajawea's role in the Lewis & Clark Expedition; Lowell Mill Girl Strikes in 1836 and 1836; teenage soldiers during the Civil War; the Mother Jones-led March of the Mill Children (1903); the Depression-era American Youth Congress and its Declaration of the Rights of American Youth; the Little Rock Nine (1957); Ruby Bridges and the struggle for school integration (1960); the Birmingham Children's Crusade (1963); the Berkeley Free Speech Movement; and the 2016 Dakota Access Pipeline Protests.

Theme-based wiki pages can also be constructed for women scientists and mathematicians, LGBTQ change makers, social and political activists, women in aviation and space exploration, and countless other topics involving how people and events connect across time periods and cultures.

INVESTIGATING SPECIAL TOPICS THROUGH INQUIRY LEARNING

Special topic wiki pages are a student-centered variation of dramatic event teaching. While special topics may or may not be required parts of local, state, or national curriculum frameworks, they are issues that students find interesting and want to explore in class. Student interest is what makes any given topic riveting, and creates the opportunity to place student questions at the center of classroom teaching and learning activities.

Inquiry learning is an instructional approach based on having students formulate and answer personally-important-to-me questions. In inquiry-based lessons, students research questions with text and digital sources, develop analyses from their findings, and share the results of their work in papers, presentations, and performances. Student inquiries are called "I Wonder Questions" because they emerge from individuals' natural curiosity about the world around them (Edwards & Maloy, 1992).

In schools, the "skill of being able to generate a wide range of questions and strategize about how to use them effectively is rarely, if ever, deliberately taught," noted educators Dan Rothstein and Luz Santana (2011). Still it is the act of asking and answering questions that "produces transformational moments to discovery and greater ownership by students of their learning." For students, the key is to be "thinking and working by asking their *own* questions, rather than responding to the questions *you* ask" (Rothstein & Santana, 2011).

Special topic wiki pages begin with questions students want to answer or issues they want to explore. Ideally, those questions or issues come spontaneously from students themselves, but questions can also come from teachers, from class discussions, or from textbooks and other readings. Whatever the source, a compelling question can spark student interest in investigating and understanding a topic. And, even when a teacher states an opening question, students can contribute additional questions that expand the initial inquiry and broaden the scope of academic learning.

The interests and questions of middle school students and their teacher in a world geography class led to the development of three sample special topic wiki pages on *Small Island Nations and Rising Sea Levels*, *Wildlife Diversity and the Serengeti Wildebeest Migration*, and *Svalbard Global Seed Bank*.

Page Examples: Small Island Nations and Rising Sea Levels, Wildlife Diversity and the Serengeti Wildebeest Migration, A Visit to the Doomsday Vault

Small Island Nations and Rising Sea Levels page:
https://resourcesforhistoryteachers.wikispaces.com/Small+Island+Nations+and+Rising+Sea+Levels,
Wildlife Diversity and the Serengeti Wildebeest Migration page:
https://resourcesforhistoryteachers.wikispaces.com/Wildlife+Diversity+and+the+Serengeti+Wildebeest+Migration,
Svalbard Global Seed Bank and the *Doomsday Vault*:
https://resourcesforhistoryteachers.wikispaces.com/A+Visit+to+the+Doomsday+Vault

Each Special Topic page was first organized around a focus question to guide inquiry-based explorations:

- *Small Island Nations and Rising Sea Levels*: What is it like to live on an island at sea level?
- *Wildlife Diversity and the Serengeti Wildebeest Migration*: Why do the Serengeti wildebeest migrate every year?
- *Svalbard Global Seed Bank*: What is so essential to life on earth that it must be stored in a secure facility near the Arctic Circle?

Starting from a focus question, special topic pages can then include: (1) Visual Images; (2) Interactive Multimedia Activities; and (3) Connections to Related Curriculum Topics.

- *Visual Images.* Pictures, photos, maps, graphs, and other visuals are a key to getting students interested in a page and its contents. The Serengeti Wildebeest Migration page includes pictures of Serengeti National Park in Kenya, blue wildebeests migrating, forest vegetation on Mount Elgon, and a 1907 book illustration of animals of Africa. The *Small Island Nations* page has pictures of the flags of Nauru and Kiribati, two of the smallest island countries, a graph of rising sea levels from 1975 to 2005, a picture of an atoll beach on Tuvalu, and a 2004 photo of a Tsunami tidal wave. Images like these engage student interest while providing information to student readers.
- *Interactive Multimedia Activities.* As they conduct inquiry-based investigations, students enjoy not only watching videos but also interacting with material on the sites they are accessing on computer, tablet, and smartphone screens. Special topic pages thus benefit from different types of interactive multimedia materials. A live Herdtracker map on the Serengeti page lets students follow herds of wildebeests as they move across the African plains. "Stop Disasters!" a serious learning game from the United Nations International Strategy for Disaster Reduction on the *Small Island Nations* page asks students to make economic and public policy choices and decisions as they engage in tsunami preparedness. Such interactive materials let students experience the topics they are investigating by multiple ways, deepening learning while sustaining inquiry as students explore and discover what is available multimodally on the page.
- *Connections to Related Curriculum Topics.* Special topic wiki pages can include connections between the page's main topic and related curricular subjects. In this way, teachers connect students' initial interests and questions to material that expands the overall academic curriculum.

The *Doomsday Vault* page about the preservation of seeds for the world's food supply includes materials about the history of famine, the origins of the foods people eat today, and the Three Sisters agricultural practices of Native Americans where corn, bean, and squash were planted and grown together.

Adding special topic material to wiki pages for individual learning standards or important history and humanities concepts promotes inquiry-based investigations in the classroom. A wiki page on an economics standard, "Explain the function of profit in a market economy," can address the principles of profit and risk for entrepreneurs and businesses and then expand to examine the topics of wealth, income, and power in American society. An American government standard on "How a bill becomes a law" can be enlarged by including special topic resources on the role of money in politics as well as the 2010 Citizens United Supreme Court decision.

Special topic pages have other advantages as well. Students can read, view, and interact with the materials already found on existing wiki pages and then add new resources from their individual and small group research. Common Core State Standards on persuasive writing, informative/exploratory texts, and personal narratives can be included on special topic pages for creative writing, poetry writing, and writing processes fit for young writers.

Students and teachers can explore important curriculum concepts by focusing on special topics related to those concepts. In geography, for example, population is a core concept, encompassing the issues facing people inhabit a place or move, voluntarily or involuntarily, to new locations. A page on the *Teaching Geography* wiki includes special topic sections on Thomas Malthus and Charles Darwin, pandemics in world history and the disappearance of civilizations for students to think about how disease, climate, and human actions impact population's growth and decline.

Teaching dramatic events and special topics engages students and deepens history and humanities learning. So does exploring the biographies of change-making individuals and reading fiction and nonfiction stories of people and places told through literature, picture books, and young adult literature as we discuss in the next chapter.

Chapter 6

Meeting People through Biographies and Books

Chinese mariner Zheng He led a vast fleet of treasure ships—the largest collection of vessels ever assembled in world history before World War I—on seven epic voyages across the Indian Ocean from Taiwan to Africa between 1405 and 1433. Born in the high mountains of Yunnan in southwest China, captured by an invading Chinese army, trained as an imperial eunuch, and triumphant as a soldier in battle, Zheng He was chosen by Zhu Di, the third emperor of the Ming Dynasty, to command China's trading armada.

Each of the treasure fleets consisted of hundreds of boats and more than 25,000 thousand sailors, soldiers, artisans, and related personnel. "All the ships of Columbus and da Gama combined," noted a National Geographic writer, "could have been stored on a single deck of a single vessel in the fleet that set sail under Zheng He" (Viviano, 2005). The voyages produced a transformative exchange of goods and ideas throughout the Indian Ocean world. At the beginning of the fifteenth century, China ruled the seas and "could have become the great colonial power a hundred years before the great age of European exploration and expansion" (Levathes, 1997, p. 20). But China turned inward after Zheng He's final voyage, leaving the world stage for centuries.

Relatively unknown among history's great explorers, Zheng He and Chinese treasure fleets highlight the importance of individuals and their stories to the study of history and humanities. Curriculum frameworks and textbooks feature prominent individuals who students are expected to know, but there are hundreds of little known and unknown history-makers who shaped events through their decisions and actions. History and biography are inseparable, said historian Ken Wolf (1994), for people's stories are a way "to keep individuals from getting lost in a panorama of social forces." For Wolf, "any chance students have of learning from the past probably depends in large part on their willingness to be fascinated by history's people."

This chapter introduces strategies for constructing wiki pages as ways to meet people students would otherwise not know about, famous people whose reputations have become memes enshrined in a cultural curriculum repeated by media and myth. Historical Biography pages illustrate the lives and times of history-making individuals. Influential Literature pages connect fiction and nonfiction books to a study of curriculum topics. The chapter finishes with descriptions of social bookmarking technologies, picture books, and young adult literature as resources for learning about people's lives and stories.

HISTORICAL IMPORTANCE AND A CULTURAL CURRICULUM

Textbooks and curriculum frameworks are populated by people deemed to be famous or important history-makers. This approach echoes the "great man" theory of history, espoused by Thomas Carlyle's 1840 dictum, "The history of the world is but the biography of great men." A great man approach is not widely championed by contemporary historians; individuals traditionally considered "great" are now viewed as the products of larger social, political, and economic forces. History is understood from the bottom-up, not just the top-down, and needs to include lives and experiences of women, people of color, and ordinary individuals often absent in classroom discussions of who is historically important.

Nevertheless, white males—presidents, American Revolutionary era figures, kings, dictators, entrepreneurs, military leaders, and economists—are the individuals most frequently named in state curriculum frameworks. In U.S. history learning standards from 1763 to 2001, the Massachusetts statewide curriculum framework specifically mentions forty-nine white men, nine African American men connected to the more than two century-long struggle for African Americans civil rights, and seven women who led the movement for women's suffrage and equality. In world history, from the fall of Rome to the present day, the Massachusetts framework mentions fifty-two European men and thirteen men from Africa, Asia, and the Americas. No women are directly named in the Massachusetts world history standards.

Those figures named in state curriculum frameworks offer teachers and students invitations to define the concepts of fame and significance in history and society. Everyone well known in our collective memory got their recognition from some source. So how did these individuals become renowned?

One answer rests in how people—young and old, students and teachers—learn about fame and significance through what Stanford University historians Sam Wineburg and Chauncey Monte-Sano (2008) call a cultural curriculum. This curriculum consists of a broad collection of images, symbols, and myths about individuals, conveyed through television, movies, advertisements, the Internet, and other media formats. Irrespective of the historical information taught in school (or whether it was taught recently or a generation ago), students and adults remember what they have learned from hearing and seeing the cultural curriculum.

The cultural curriculum concept informs Wineburg and Monte-Sano's (2008) "Famous Americans" paper reporting how high school students and everyday Americans think about and identify who is important in history. Noting that new editions of history textbooks are offering more inclusive coverage of people in history, the two historians wondered if "presented with a page of blank lines, whom would today's high school students list as the most famous individuals from American history?" (Weinburg & Monte-Sano, 2008, p. 1188).

Two thousand 11th and 12th graders in schools from all fifty states were asked to list names of the most famous Americans in history "from Columbus to the present day." The sole rule was no presidents could be included on the lists. Then the same students were asked to list the most famous women in American history. No wives of presidents could be on this list. The students were enrolled in public high schools broadly representative nationally in terms of racial and ethnic makeup, selection of academic course offerings, and number of students receiving free lunch. As a comparison, 2,000 American-born adults, aged forty-five and older, were asked to construct the same two lists.

Dr. Martin Luther King, Jr., the highest-ranking individual in the survey, was listed by 67 percent of the students. Rosa Parks (60 percent) was followed by Harriet Tubman (44 percent), Susan B. Anthony (34 percent), Benjamin Franklin (29 percent), Amelia Earhart (23 percent), Oprah Winfrey (22 percent), Marilyn Monroe (19 percent), Thomas Edison (18 percent), and Albert Einstein (16 percent). Differences reflected backgrounds: "Black students were nearly three times more likely than white students to name King, twice as likely as whites to name Tubman and Oprah Winfrey, and 1.5 times as likely to name Parks" (Weinburg & Monte-Sano, 2008, p. 1191).

Seeing the adult lists, the historians were surprised to find a "remarkable overlap" with those of the students (Weinburg & Monte-Sano, 2008, p. 1191). Eight of the ten most named figures were identical (Betsy Ross and Henry Ford replaced Marilyn Monroe and Albert Einstein). Why, asked the historians, were "different generations and different races congregated around five or six common names with astounding consistency?" (Weinburg & Monte-Sano, 2008, p. 1198).

Wineburg and Monte-Sano concluded that the cultural curriculum communicates broad views about historical figures that have lasting power in people's memories. For example, within the cultural curriculum, Rosa Parks is widely but inaccurately remembered as an "unassuming old lady (she was forty-two years old) whose only thought was resting her tired feet after a long day on the job and whose humble and courageous act of defiance single-handedly sparked the bus boycott that led to the end of segregation and Jim Crow" (Weinburg & Monte-Sano, 2008, p. 1201). The truth is that Rosa Parks was not a solitary, one-time actor. She was a lifelong committed political activist whose refusal to leave her seat was part of a planned NAACP action against segregation in public transportation. There were other riders before her who had refused to give up their seats; after months of planning it was Rosa Parks' actions that became the catalyst for the Montgomery Bus Boycott.

Widespread and deeply entrenched, the cultural curriculum forms the basis for how people of all ages and generations remember stories of the past. Expanding the cultural curriculum to include the actions of lesser known, but socially, culturally, politically, and economically important individuals is an ongoing challenge for teachers and students learning history and humanities.

REPUTATIONS AS MEMES

A different explanation for how individuals gain prominence in society and curriculum is based on the concept of memes, "simple ideas that reproduce when spread from mind to mind." By their shared nature, memes function as "capsule summaries that make them easy to remember" (Skiena & Ward, 2013, pp. 4, 13). Because memes are endlessly repeated in and out of school, Betsy Ross is remembered as designer and seamstress of the first American flag, and Paul Revere is celebrated as the fearless patriot who rode through every Middlesex village and town warning the colonists that the British were coming. Evidence to the contrary, as well as the activities and accomplishments of other individuals, do not rise to the same level of significance in people's minds because of the oft-told memories shared by so many.

As memes, historical figures are "occupying niches in history, analogous to how species thrive in particular ecological systems," conclude statisticians Steve Skiena and Charles Ward in their book, *Who's Bigger: Where Historical Figures Really Rank* (2013, p. 4). Reputations rise or fall over time as events impact "our collective memory to determine which figures get preserved for posterity." Jesus, Napoleon, Muhammad, William Shakespeare, Abraham Lincoln, George Washington, Adolf Hitler, Aristotle, Alexander the Great, and Thomas Jefferson ranked from one to ten in Skiena and Ward's list of the one hundred most significant historical figures (2013, p. 6).

To create rankings of people's significance, Skiena and Ward (2013, p. 19) mined data from the English-language version of Wikipedia to integrate a "diverse set of measurements about their reputation into a single consensus value." The first measure was "PageRank" or the number of pages in Wikipedia that are linked to a person's page on the site. "Web Hits," the number of times a page is visited, was a second measure. In theory, important people's pages will be visited more often than pages of less important people. "Article length" was a third measure—longer articles, written by multiple contributors, signify a person's greater importance. A fourth measure, "Page Edits," assumes that important individuals will have pages edited more often and more thoroughly.

Significance emerges as the "result of social and cultural forces acting on the mass of an individual's achievement" (Skiena & Ward, 2013, p. 3), including

- *Founder Effects:* People remember individuals such as explorers or inventors whose memes establish that person as the first to do something now considered to be an enduring achievement—whether the person was in fact the first or not. For example, Christopher Columbus supersedes Leif Ericson or other Viking explorers as the first European to "discover" America.
- *Role Replacement:* Newer historical figures regularly replace older individuals in people's historical memory. In that past fifty years, the "meme of the 'greatest living saint' has been transferred from Albert Schweitzer to Mother Teresa to the Dalai Lama" (Skiena and Ward, 2013, p. 12).
- *Narrative Simplification:* People remember fewer historical figures from long-ago events. Of the organizers who made possible the 1963 March on Washington for Jobs and Freedom, Bayard Rustin, A. Philip Randolph, Roy Wilkins, John Lewis, James Farmer, Whitney Young, Jr. and Ralph Abernathy are less well known than Martin Luther King, Jr. as leaders of the March.
- *Storification:* People are more likely to remember individuals whose lives contain a compelling storyline or feature a memorable moment in history. Patrick Henry's "Give me liberty, or give me death" speech makes him a widely recognized American revolutionary era figure while John Adams, quietly notable as the first vice president, second president, and father of the sixth president, is not as often touted or quoted.

There are inherent problems in this approach, as Skiena and Ward readily admit. In the Wikipedia rankings, men have more prominence than women; whites are more remembered than people of color; contemporary figures are relatively overvalued; and Americans are overrepresented in comparison to individuals from other regions and cultures in the world. It is also difficult to distinguish between historical gravitas (those who substantively impacted people and events) and contemporary celebrity (those who are known for their short-term but inconsequential actions in modern society).

The pervasiveness of the cultural curriculum and the idea that people's reputations exist as memes demand that students and teachers ask questions about fame and significance. Those who read and contribute to Wikipedia, or any other ranking of historical or contemporary importance, mainly write about individuals they know, and these are the people who are included in textbooks, frameworks, and curriculum. For this reason, uncovering the stories of women and men who have been omitted from the lists is an essential step in building a more inclusive history and humanities curriculum. As little known and long-neglected lives and stories are discovered and discussed, the historical record is broadened and diversified.

HISTORICAL BIOGRAPHY WIKI PAGES

Historical biography wiki pages highlight the life and times of real figures in history—the well-known and often taught *and* the rarely taught whose stories uncover and discover the past. Historical biography pages utilize the same online resource categories as Dramatic Event pages (primary sources, multimedia and multicultural materials, and teaching/learning resources) and include links to information about a person's life from multiple sources such as online biographies from educational organizations, obituaries from the *New York Times* or other newspapers, and multimedia resources such as Google Doodle pages, YouTube videos or podcasts by scholars.

Page Example: Helen Keller

Visit *Helen Keller Historical Biography* page:
https://resourcesforhistoryteachers.wikispaces.com/Helen+Keller

Social and disability rights activist Helen Keller offers a model for building historical biography wiki pages. While widely cited for her heroic efforts to overcome the isolation inherent in being deaf and blind, Helen Keller is less known for her lifelong political activism. She joined the Socialist Party in 1909, helped to found the American Civil Liberties Union, supported the birth control movement, and wrote essays advocating women's suffrage and radical economic change (Loewen, 2007, pp. 12–15). Her Historical Biography page includes the following elements:

- *Online Biography*: Biographies from American Foundation for the Blind and Helen Keller Kids Online Museum.
- *Visual Images*: 1912 Photograph of Helen Keller from the Library of Congress; 2003 image of Helen Keller on the reverse side of the Alabama state

quarter; and a picture of a hand forming the letters A-S-L for American Sign Language—each serves to highlight different aspects of her life's story.

- ***Primary Sources***: *The Story of My Life* (1905), an autobiography she began writing when she was twenty-two years old and now published as an e-book by the University of Pennsylvania; an essay, *How I Became a Socialist* (1912); selected pages from Helen Keller's FBI Files; and *Why I Became an IWW* (1916) from the International Workers of the World website—each offers insights into Helen Keller's political activism and the responses of the government to her activities.
- ***Multimedia Resources***: "Helen Keller Speech," an historical reenactment of a speech she gave to the 1925 Lions Club International Convention on YouTube from Lions International; "Helen Keller & Anne Sullivan," 1930s newsreel footage also on YouTube; and "Helen Keller Tribute Film" from Connecticut Women's Hall of Fame—each multimedia resource shows different ways to depict her life.
- ***Multicultural History***: "The Radical Dissent of Helen Keller" (Yes! Magazine, July 12, 2012) describes her political activism.
- ***Lesson Plans and Teaching Ideas***: "Exploring Disability Using Multimedia and the B-D-A Reading Strategy" is an interactive learning experience from the National Council of English's ReadWriteThink website.

FROM KNOWN TO LESS WELL-KNOWN INDIVIDUALS

Historical Biography wiki pages can be used to expand curriculum from known to less well-known individuals. In this approach, a well-known figure (someone featured in textbooks or frameworks) is the starting point for the study of individuals or groups omitted or underdiscussed in curriculum frameworks and textbooks—either within a given time period or across multiple time periods. The untold stories of nineteenth- and twentieth-century African American inventors contrasted with the often-told story of Eli Whitney and the 1794 invention of the cotton gin serves as an example of using Historical Biography wiki pages to move the curriculum from known to less well-known individuals.

Page Example: Eli Whitney and the Development of the Cotton Gin

Visit the *Eli Whitney* page:
https://resourcesforhistoryteachers.wikispaces.com/Eli+Whitney+and+the+Development+of+the+Cotton+Gin

The cotton gin was a revolutionary technology. Prior to its invention, laborers had to pick seeds from harvested cotton by hand. With Whitney's machine, seeds could be removed from cotton at rates far exceeding what humans could do on their own. By mechanizing cotton harvesting, the cotton gin revitalized the southern planation economy, prolonged African American slavery, and contributed to the intersectional divisions that led to the Civil War.

As the story of Whitney's invention is often told, inspirational genius led him to create the cotton gin, as in this text from the Eli Whitney Museum and Workshop website: "At the urging of Mrs. Green and Phineas Miller, Whitney watched the cotton cleaning and studied the hand movements. One hand held the seed while the other hand teased out the short strands of lint. The machine he designed simply duplicated this" (Wilson, 1954).

But multiple untold stories surround Eli Whitney's invention. Cotton gins were a long-standing technology, having been used "to remove cotton fiber from the seed since the first century of the common era," noted historian Angela Lakwete (2003, p. 1). These early gins were located on "three continents, in Asia, Africa, and the American Southwest, where Native Americans cultivated *G. hirsutum* [upland or Mexican cotton]" (Lakwete, 2003, p. 3). Whitney essentially built on earlier technology and other inventors subsequently improved his design by creating the saw gin whose adoption in the "mid-1820s coincided with the social and economic upheavals that shaped antebellum America" (Lakwete, 2003, p. ix).

Page Example: African American Inventors

Visit *African American Inventors* Page:
https://resourcesforhistoryteachers.wikispaces.com/African+American+Inventors

The untold stories of African American inventors throughout U.S. history offer a dramatic counterpoint to the story of Eli Whitney and the invention of the cotton gin. Because they were denied citizenship before the Civil War, African slaves could not patent any invention. But slaves made significant contributions: "Onesimus, a Massachusetts slave owned by Puritan leader Cotton Mather, is credited with making a remedy for smallpox that was introduced in 1721. Another Massachusetts slave, Ebar, invented a broom made from broomcorn around 1800" (Schons, 2011). John H. Lienhard (1988), reporting on the University of Houston's *Engines of Our Ingenuity* radio program, cites evidence that Jo Anderson, a slave, worked with Cyrus McCormick on the invention of the mechanical reaper while a slave named Benjamin Montgomery designed a new screw propeller for steamboats.

To realize their visions for change, African American inventors had to confront powerful racism and persistent prejudice. In 1821, Thomas L. Jennings, inventor and black abolitionist, was the first African American freeman to receive a patent for a forerunner to modern-day dry-cleaning process (Johnson, 2011). Notable African American inventors include Henry Blair (harvester technology); Norbert Rillieux (sugar refining evaporator); Elijah McCoy (oil-dripping cup); Sarah E. Goode (folding cabinet bed); Garrett Morgan (a gas mask and the automated traffic signal); Jan Matzeliger (shoe sewing machine); and Granville Woods—the so-called Black Edison who invented the third rail for subway trains along with dozens of other innovations (Turner, 2008).

There is the history of Benjamin Banneker, a largely self-taught mathematician, astronomer, and inventor whose accomplishments include a clock made from three-dimensional wooden parts, a central role in the design of the nation's capital in Washington, D.C., and the publishing of an annual Almanac he wrote and for which he did all the scientific calculations. Banneker was an outspoken advocate for African American rights, directly challenging Thomas Jefferson's stated beliefs of the inferiority of black people.

The *African American Inventors* wiki page connects to occasions of technological change throughout U.S. history: the emergence of the American system of manufacturing with interchangeable parts in New England's mid-nineteenth-century textile mills; the early twentieth-century introduction of the assembly line in the mass production of automobiles; and the late twentieth-century computer and communication revolution. In each case, often told stories create a framework for exploring the untold stories of not only African American inventors, but women inventors and inventors from other diverse groups.

BIOGRAPHY COLLAGES USING SOCIAL BOOKMARKING

Social bookmarking, a flexible and accessible information organization technology, offers a way to broaden the study of historically important individuals while teaching students more ways to navigate the complexities of online information. Briefly defined, social bookmarking involves "saving bookmarks to a public website and 'tagging' them with keywords" (Educause Learning Initiative, 2005).

Social bookmarking combines private bookmarking (where computer users save URLs on a personal computer to revisit later) with social media (where computer users save their URLs to the cloud, then share their bookmarks with others who in turn share their bookmarks as part of a network of shared users). Popular social bookmarking programs include Diigo (Digest of Internet Information, Groups, and Other Stuff), LiveBinder, Scoop.it, or Pinterest.

Social bookmarking enables students and teachers to assemble "biography collages," wide-ranging collections of materials and perspectives about individuals and events in history, including sources from the people themselves. In creating a biography collage, the goal is not to stop after locating a single text-based biography such as those found on Wikipedia or other online biography sites, but to construct a collage of information about an individual's life, times, impacts, and lasting legacies. Once assembled and saved online, these resources invigorate classroom activities and transform content-specific wiki pages from text-only to multimodal learning opportunities.

Students and teachers begin social bookmarking by "tagging" resources they find online. A tag is a self-chosen keyword that helps generate a unique information management structure known as a "folksonomy." Rather than relying on keywords created by other people, a folksonomy puts social bookmarkers in charge of the research experience. Students, after all, are more likely to care about and remember terms they create for themselves. Tagging also shows the importance of creating keywords so other people can find information when they search online. The keyword "war" is so broad that it will not immediately direct web searchers to individual curriculum topics such as World War I, trench warfare, the Battle of Verdun, or the Harlem Hellfighters.

Once web resources have been located and tagged, they can be grouped together to create a biography collage about a person or a group. In Diigo, a bundle of related resources is referred to as an "outliner." Different types of resources—secondary sources, primary sources, multimedia sources, and teaching materials—make up a biography collage and that can then be used to create an historical biography wiki page.

Page Example: Bessie Coleman

> Visit *Bessie Coleman* page:
> https://resourcesforhistoryteachers.wikispaces.com/Bessie+Coleman

Bessie Coleman, the early twentieth-century aviator, stunt flyer, and first African American woman to hold an international pilot's license, offers a model for generating an historical biography collage of social bookmarked resources for building an historical biography wiki page. Bessie Coleman's story features her struggles to overcome racial and gender discrimination in the field of aviation, saving to go to Paris to learn French and study for her pilot's license, and then voicing outspoken opposition to African American segregation in the South where as an aerial show performer she refused to appear before white-only audiences.

Bessie Coleman's tag bundle on the Delicious social bookmarking site features biographies from the Atlanta Historical Museum and the U.S. Centennial of Flight Commission (secondary source); a 1921 newspaper article and promotional billboard about her aerial shows (primary source); a U.S. postage stamp issued in 1991 to honor Coleman's accomplishments (visual source); and an online learning game from the PBS FlyGirls website (interactive source). The tag bundle comprises two other resources: an essay on Coleman from the book *Realizing the Dream of Flight* and a lesson plan that uses the struggles of black aviators to explore campaigns for social change. These materials are featured in Bessie Coleman's historical biography page on the *resourcesforhistoryteachers* wiki.

Once assembled, biography collages can be linked to specific curriculum learning standards. Bessie Coleman's life could illustrate a standard calling for students and teachers to "analyze the post-Civil War struggles of African Americans and women to gain basic civil rights" (Massachusetts Department of Education, 2003, p. 74).

Biography collages of multiple individuals can link to the same learning standard. For instance, biography collages for nineteenth-century women scientists Ada Lovelace, Mary Anning, Caroline Herschel, Mary Sommerville, Maria Mitchell, Beatrice Potter, and Elizabeth Blackwell become learning resources for AP World History Key Concept 5.1, subpart VI.B that asks students to explore "family dynamics, gender roles, and demographics changed in response to industrialization." Women who made important contributions to science in the twentieth century—Grace Hopper, Barbara McClintock, Irene Joliot-Curie, Hedy Lamarr, and Margaret Sanger—inform AP World History Key Concept 6.1, subpart B that focuses how on "new scientific paradigms transformed human understanding of the world."

INCORPORATING PICTURE BOOKS AND YOUNG ADULT LITERATURE

By engaging readers visually, emotionally, and intellectually, picture books and young adult literature become classroom learning and wiki building resources. Artwork and photography produce memorable images that complement the written text; language and narrative make these materials accessible to students with different reading levels and background knowledge. Stories told through picture books and young adult literature transport readers into other times and places, revealing life as it is lived by people and raising questions about why individuals and groups did what they did in response to the conditions and struggles they were facing.

The National Council for the Social Studies' (NCSS) yearly selection of Notable Social Studies Trade Books for Young People is a wide-ranging source of picture book and young adult stories about people and events that relate to curriculum learning standards. The NCSS selections, published online since 2000, list books in multiple historical and humanities categories, including biographies, contemporary concerns, the environment/energy/ecology, folk-tales, geography, historical life in the Americas, and world history and culture.

In addition to the NCSS selections, students and teachers can access books for young readers that have received a Newbery or Caldecott Medal and Honor, Coretta Scott King Book Award, Carter G. Woodson Award, Jane Addams Book Award, Tomas Rivera Mexican American Children's Book Award, American Indian Youth Award, Arab American Book Award, and Asian Pacific American Award for Literature. There are also noteworthy book selections made by the American Library Association, the International Literacy Association, and other educational and literacy organizations.

Here are three ways to use picture books and young adult literature as part of teacher- and student-made educational wikis: (1) as sources of historical biographies of less known and unknown figures in history; (2) as resources for teaching specific learning standards; and (3) as text sets offering multiple perspectives about events.

Picture Book Biographies

In selecting biographies for its notable book lists, NCSS blends titles about well-known persons with the stories of individuals who despite their accomplishments are rarely discussed in history and humanities classes. Between 2014 and 2016, NCSS chose picture book and young adult biographies about prominent historical figures including Abraham Lincoln, Frederick Douglass, Harriet Tubman, Theodore Roosevelt, the Beatles, Anne Frank, Benjamin Franklin, Nelson Mandela, Albert Einstein, Robert Frost, Beatrix Potter, Muhammad Ali, and Dr. Paul Farmer.

At the same time, NCSS featured books about less well-known women and men whose lives reveal historical issues and cultural tensions: the woman astronomer Henrietta Leavitt; the astronaut Sally Ride; early twentieth-century actress and aviation pioneer Ruth Elder; Hip Hop music pioneer DJ Kool Herc; jazz musicians Trombone Shorty, Charlie "Bird" Parker and John "Dizzy" Gillespie; the Pakistani education rights activist Malala Yousafzai; Victorian-era photographer Julia Margaret Cameron; early twentieth-century investigative journalist Elizabeth Cochrane (Nelly Bly) as well as other women war correspondents and photojournalists; African American slave Philip Reid who was instrumental in getting the statute of freedom to its place atop the U.S. Capitol dome; and John Roy Lynch, who born into slavery, became the Speaker of the Mississippi House of Representatives and U.S. Congressman in the decades after the Civil War.

As they build wiki pages, students and teachers can locate information about individuals found in textbooks and frameworks and then add the stories of less well-known individuals as told through picture books and young adult literature. In this way, learning standards and historical events are expanded to include women and men whose actions contributed to the social and cultural change. Stories of historical and modern-day change agents add depth and complexity to standards by focusing students' attention on people's actions in society's transformations.

Linking Books, Standards, and Events

Picture books and young adult literature can be linked to learning standards and to important events that are part of or extend from those standards. *A Death-Struck Year*, Makiia Lucier's story of a young girl who volunteers in a Portland, Oregon hospital during the 1918 Influenza Pandemic, can be read in conjunction with an AP world history standard on how disease, scientific innovations, and conflicts led to demographic shifts in the twentieth century. *Brave Girl: Clara and the Shirtwaist Makers' Strike of 1909* by Michelle Markel, the story of Clara Lemlich, leader of the largest strike of women workers in U.S. history, relates to standards on the formation of unions during the Industrial era. *A Single Pebble: A Story of the Silk Road* is Bonnie Christensen's tale of how a small jade stone, sent by a young girl in China, travels the length of the Silk Road to a young boy in Venice, Italy and connects directly to standards about political, economic, and religious developments one of the major periods of Islamic history.

Sometimes, books extend the scope of standards across time periods, as with *Ninth Ward*, Jewel Parker Rhodes' 2010 novel about twelve-year-old Lanesha and her family living in New Orleans during Hurricane Katrina that reveals the poverty and discrimination still facing African Americans in the South half-a-century after the Civil Rights Movement.

Page Example: Ninth Ward

Visit the *Ninth Ward* Page:
https://teachingresourcesforenglish.wikispaces.com/Ninth+Ward

On August 29, 2005, Hurricane Katrina came ashore in New Orleans with sustained winds of 125 mph. Immense destruction followed when the levees failed; some 80 percent of the city had water in the streets and homes. Particularly devastated were the largely African American sections of St. Bernard Parish and the Ninth Ward. More than 2,000 people were killed; tens of thousands displaced from their homes; damage was estimated at $108 billion.

Through characters that readers care about, Parker Rhodes' novel forces students to consider the immensity of the event and the tragedy of the storm and its aftermath. A wiki page about the book can be designed to support interdisciplinary teaching and learning activities, for as teacher Mike Roberts (2012, p. 95) has noted, a key advantage of young adult literature is how it can "help students connect with and better understand what they are learning in class."

The *Ninth Ward* book wiki page has links to websites about the book, its author and how to study the characters and the plot, but also includes meteorological information about hurricanes in general and Katrina in particular that can be used in science and math classes. The page has social studies-related material about how decisions made by the Army Corps of Engineers to save money during dam construction led to the failure of the levees to protect the city from massive flooding. There are also links to the resources describing in detail the larger history of the city with its place in American and African American music, society, and culture. In this way, a wiki page for a single book is utilized across the curriculum, its characters and stories making language arts, science, math, and social studies content more meaningfully real for students.

Building Text Sets

Text sets are a way to add multiple stories to wiki pages, awakening readers' understandings of people and events. To create a text set, students and teachers locate fiction and nonfiction books that address an historical or contemporary event and post them on a learning standard or dramatic event wiki page. The internment of Japanese Americans during World War II can be explored through *Fish for Jimmy*, Katie Yamasaki; *Baseball Saved Us*, Ken Mochizuki; *Barbed Wire Baseball*, Marissa Moss; and *Imprisoned: The Betrayal of Japanese Americans during World War II*, Martin W. Sandler.

The Underground Railroad can be viewed through *Follow the Drinking Gourd*, Jeanette Winter; *Henry's Freedom Box*, Ellen Levine; *Under the Freedom Tree*; *Running Out of Night*, Sharon Lovejoy; *Harriet Tubman: Conductor on the Underground Railroad*, Ann Petry; and *The Price of Freedom: How One Town Stood Up to Slavery*, Dennis Brindell Fradin & Judith Bloom Fradin.

The goal of a text set is to create an accessible wide-angle view of people and events, including voices and stories that are not usually part of those textbooks and frameworks. Individuals or small learning groups read the books and report to peers how the stories add to their understanding of society. A text set, like a wiki, continues to expand as students add new books to the list.

INFLUENTIAL LITERATURE WIKI PAGES

Influential Literature wiki pages connect books to events and themes in history and humanities curriculum. These pages can feature novels, stage plays, poetry, nonfiction studies, or investigative reports. Reading in multiple genres, students think about historical and contemporary issues, topics, and decisions "in the context of the story and its characters" rather than solely from their own experience and perspective (Dever, Sorenson, & Broderick, 2005). Here are two influential literature wiki page examples, one from adult literature and the other from young adult fiction, where books and their themes are linked to learning standards and curriculum topics.

Page Example: The Grapes of Wrath

> Visit *The Grapes of Wrath* Page:
> https://teachingresourcesforenglish.wikispaces.com/The+Grapes+of+Wrath

The Grapes of Wrath, John Steinbeck's 1939 Pulitzer Prize-winning novel about the Dust Bowl, offers a model for organizing an Influential Literature wiki page based on a work of fiction. Posted on *Teaching Resources for English*, the page is cross-linked to history standards for the Great Depression and the New Deal and has the following components:

- ***Book Synopsis and Author Biography***: Book Summary from the National Steinbeck Center and a Brief Biography from NoblePrize.org.
- ***Visual Images***: First Edition Book Cover; photograph of John Steinbeck, 1962; Dust Bowl Photograph, 1936; and a photograph of Henry Fonda as Tom Joad in the movie version of the book collectively offer a wide-ranging visual context for the book.

- **Primary Sources**: A *New York Times* Book Review of the novel, April 16, 1939, and *The Grapes of Wrath* by John Steinbeck Primary Source Set from Digital Public Library of America.
- **Multimedia Resources**: *Grapes of Wrath* original movie trailer (1940); "*Grapes of Wrath* Book Covers: A Short History" from the blog, 101 Books.
- **Multicultural History**: Resources on 1965–1970 Delano Grape Strike and Boycott by Filipino American Farmworkers in California.
- **Lesson Plans and Teaching Ideas**: "Film Study of *The Grapes of Wrath*" from the New Deal Network's Great Depression and the Arts website.

Influential literature wiki pages can also be created for young adult literature (YA). The appeal of these books is that they have been "written *about* adolescents, *with adolescent readers in mind*" (Groenke & Scherff, 2010, p. 2). High-quality YA books focus on young people's lives and experiences, showing characters "dealing with life on their own terms as best they could" as "capable, smart and multidimensional" individuals (Groenke & Scherff, 2010, p. xii).

STRATEGIES FOR STUDENTS AND TEACHERS

There are six strategies for building Historical Biography and Influential Literature wiki pages. First, adopt a consistent framework for organizing online information. Teachers might choose our suggested categories—primary sources, secondary sources, audio/visual resources, interactive resources, and other materials—or create categories of their own. The goal is to locate a range of resources that convey a broad portrait of a person's life or present an expansive view of key literature in the context of a social and historical time period.

Second, expand the Internet research process from text-only to multimedia and multimodal resources. Using technology, students and teachers are able to locate primary and secondary sources (which are often text-based) and visual and interactive sources as well. Photographs, artwork, motion pictures, sound recordings, maps, posters, and other multimedia resources are then brought to the center of history and humanities education. Students actively learn through personal research rather than passively listening to a teacher's oral presentations.

Third, encourage students to take a wide-angle look at people and events (Shaw, n.d.). Rather than compressing the life and times of an historical figure or the plot of a story into a short text-based account like those often found in school textbooks or on encyclopedia websites, wiki pages expand perspectives through the inclusion of multicultural and multimedia online resources. People's lives are then viewed less in terms of names, dates, and places and more in terms of issues and themes raised by their actions. On Bessie Coleman's page, for example, students meet the first African American international female pilot who was a history-changing individual struggling to overcome segregation and improve society—themes that resonate within all history and humanities curriculum.

Fourth, link Historical Biography and Influential Literature pages to multiple learning standards.

- *The Crucible*, Arthur Miller's play recounting the Salem Witch Trials can be connected not only to standards about colonial America but also the McCarthy Red Scare of the 1950s.
- *The Prince*, Machiavelli's classic study of the exercising of political power can be connected to standards about the Renaissance and the formation of American government.
- *The Jungle*, Upton Sinclair's muckraking expose of the early twentieth-century meatpacking industry can be connected to standards about the Progressive era in American politics along with contemporary efforts to improve consumer and health safety.
- *All Quiet on the Western Front*, Erich Maria Remarque's timeless antiwar novel can be connected to standards on World War I and other conflicts occurring today.
- *1984* and *Animal Farm*, George Orwell's dystopian novels can be connected to standards about the rise of totalitarianism in the twentieth century.

Fifth, connecting books to standards does not mean that students must read the entire text as part of class learning activities. There is not enough time in the school year for such in-depth, college seminar-like study of individual books. But students can experience literature in different, yet dynamics ways by reading excerpts by themselves or a part of a readers' theater presentation; watching video segments from movie, television, or stage adaptation; acting out scenes in class; or writing new versions of the story with modern-day characters, situations, and settings. The key is for literature to expand students' view of history and society.

Finally, the building historical biography and influential literature wiki pages promotes the transforming how teaching and learning happens in classrooms. By assembling a collection of links about historical figures or important books, new information is created that widens the discussion of the past and its implications for the present and the future. By sharing that information digitally, students and teachers affirm their membership in wider communities of school, community, nation, and world—each of which can benefit from what students are learning. Gaining and sharing information supports the goal of preparing students to be digital literate members of a twenty-first century democratic society. All these outcomes are further supported by the instructional changes generated by "flipped learning," by an online learning strategy called "WikiQuests," and by students assuming active roles as contributors to the development of wiki pages, the focus of the final chapter in this book.

Chapter 7

Engaging Students Using Flipped Learning

This book features ideas and strategies for using wikis to transform history and humanities learning across grade levels. Wikis incorporate technology-based instruction, multimedia and multicultural resources, and active learning to teach standards-based curriculum. Wikis reveal hidden histories, untold stories, dramatic events, historical biographies, and special academic topics. Wikis engage students in learning new literacy skills, collaborating with adults and peers, developing critical thinking, and experiencing thematic teaching. This final chapter shows how wikis can flip classroom learning to student-centered instructional approaches.

Flipped learning is an instructional approach where students gain knowledge about academic topics outside of class from videos and digital materials while in class they do projects or solve problems individually and in small groups with the guidance of a teacher (Bergmann & Sams, 2012, 2014, 2015). Like wikis, flipped learning is technology based, providing a means to actively involve students in reading, viewing, hearing, and analyzing web-based materials and giving them opportunities to post content they write or create.

An example of a wiki creating flipped learning is reflected in one middle school geography class's annual staging of a World Forum activity. This variation of the Model UN (United Nations) simulation has students become representatives of global issues instead of individual countries. Students envision of the world as collections of interdependent communities; document global social and economic problems; propose solutions based on individual, national, and international actions; and conduct discussions democratically in a forum of representative student voices and leadership.

The World Forum begins with students discussing and cataloging what they think are paramount issues facing people of the world today: women's rights, world hunger and poverty, climate change and global warming, protection of wildlife diversity, water use, and environmental protection—to name some of the recently proposed topics. Through consensus decision-making, students select the four or five issues they deem most important to discuss in the World Forum.

Students choose one of the topics and in small groups begin researching it. As they locate, evaluate, and select resources about the topics, groups build a new page or post material to an existing page in the *resourceforhistoryteachers* or *Teaching Geography* wikis. Publishing on the wiki accomplishes two flipped learning goals. First, when the World Forum convenes, anyone can access information about the issues from the online pages rather than listen to a teacher presentation about a topic. Second, the resources add to students' knowledge of expository writing and proposal design as members of the class hear about each group's ideas for collective action, such as creating public service announcements, conducting fund drives to support a cause, or soliciting signatures for written petitions.

Beginning with the World Forum example, this chapter explores ways of using wikis to create flipped learning instructional practices: wikis functioning as tech books and teacher- and student-made collections of web resources chosen to fit the needs and interests of individual classes; wikis as interactive learning experiences with questions for students to answer as they view and interact with online material as part of homework assignments; WikiQuests as an instructional approach where students explore academic topics using teacher-chosen online resources; and wiki pages as online publishing venues for students to be active contributors of multimedia and multicultural learning resources.

DEFINING FLIPPED LEARNING

Broadly speaking, flipped learning reverses "the typical lecture and homework elements of a course" (Educause Learning Initiative, 2012). Instead of teachers using lectures, discussions, and PowerPoint presentations to convey information during face-to-face class time, students use computers and handheld technologies to access assigned information on their own outside of class. When the class meets, the "resulting group space is transformed into a dynamic, interactive learning environment where the educator guides students as they apply concepts and engage creatively in the subject matter" (Flipped Learning Network, 2014).

Enabled by the wide availability of mobile devices, flipped learning is gaining prominence in higher education. College and university courses from physics, marketing, health, and nursing to engineering and history are using forms of technology-based flipped instruction. Students watch online videos and use multiple digital resources outside of class, while during class they work individually or in small groups to apply concepts, solve problems, and apply academic content.

By shifting what happens instructionally before and during class time, flipped learning upends a model of schooling that has dominated American education for more than one hundred years—teachers as transmitters of knowledge; students as passive receivers of information. Teacher-centered instruction has been remarkably resistant to change. As historian Larry Cuban (1993, p. 18) noted, "Approaches where students work together, move freely around the room, and determine tasks for themselves" are largely incompatible with teacher-centered classrooms. Historically, concluded Cuban, few teachers have been "willing to upset their controlled, familiar world for the uncertain benefits of a student-centered classroom."

To date, direct instruction in flipped learning classes has been delivered "usually—though not exclusively—through teacher-created videos" (Bergmann & Sams, 2014). Wikis, however, enable students and teachers to access wide-ranging collections of multimodal academic content during the outside-of-class component of flipped instruction. Students read, listen, watch, and interact with online resources before class, creating the time and space for more interactive, collaborative in-class learning experiences.

In flipping a course, higher education faculties have situations that differ from most K–12 teachers. College classes meet two or three times a week rather than everyday so students have more time to do work outside of class to prepare for in-class activities. Colleges have extensive technology resources, including classrooms with multiple laptop computers on circular tables to encourage small group work; flat screen monitors connected to a central instructional station to facilitate visual communications among class members; and digital projectors, lecture capture technology, and surround sound audio systems to promote interaction among students and the teacher. K–12 school technology is usually not as extensive. So instead of a large-scale reorganization of curriculum and instruction across an entire college semester, K–12 teachers and students can think in terms of class time spent using wikis to support flipped lessons and interactive learning.

In flipped learning lessons at the elementary, middle, and high school levels, students, after completing outside-of-class assignments, work individually and in small groups during class to create presentations, performances, or portfolios to show what they are learning. There is less teacher-centered instruction and more student-centered activities, shown in the following examples, each using wikis as a key technology in flipping the structure of teaching and learning: (1) wikis as a tech book; (2) online assignments with questions for students; (3) WikiQuests; and (4) students making regular contributions to wiki pages.

WIKIS AS TECH BOOKS

Digital textbooks, available as free online open educational resources (OERs), are emerging as alternatives to expensive paperbound books in K–12 schools as well as colleges and universities (WikiEducator, 2010). One leading OER provider, the Open Textbook Library from the Center for Open Education at the University of Minnesota, offers peer-reviewed textbooks in multiple subject areas that can be downloaded for free or printed at low cost, including a U.S. history text with topics from precolonial America to the present day and an American government book dealing with the foundations of the U.S. political system, available from OpenStax College online.

Multiple websites also offer OER history and humanities content including "Digital History" from the University of Houston, "U.S. History: Pre-Columbian to the New Millennium" from the Independence Hall Association in Philadelphia, "History by Era" from the Gilder Lehrman Institute of American History, "America's Story" from the Library of Congress, "North Carolina History: A Digital Textbook" from the University of North Carolina, "Ancient Civilizations" from Independence Hall Association in Philadelphia, "World History for All of Us" from San Diego State University, and "e-History" from The Ohio State University. A listing of digital resources for history content is available online.

Page Examples: Digital Resources for History Content

Visit *Open Stax College*
http://open.umn.edu/opentext- books/BookDetail.aspx?bookId=206
Visit *Listing of Digital Textbooks*
https://resourcesforhistoryteachers. wikispaces.com/Listing+of+Digital+ Textbooks

Both open education digital textbooks and paper textbooks have important limitations as instructional tools. They may not address individual local or state learning standards or encompass themes or topics that teachers want to explore with students. They may not include the hidden histories and untold stories of diverse individuals and groups or focus on dramatic events and works of influential literature.

By contrast, a wiki used as a digital "tech book" can provide multicultural and multimodal resources chosen by teachers and students. Wiki pages on *resourcesforhistoryteachers*, *Teaching Resources for English,* and *Teaching Geography* offer text, video, audio, interactive websites and timelines, online learning games, virtual reality simulations, and historical animations and visualizations. By featuring interactions beyond reading printed text and viewing static images, multimodal tech book activities offer choice in flipped learning experience for students.

A wiki page on the Great Depression and the New Deal and a page exploring the topic of Population in a Geography class offer examples of how teacher- and student-developed wikis function as a tech book for flipped learning.

Page Example: The Great Depression and the New Deal

> Visit the *Great Depression and the New Deal* page:
> https://resourcesforhistoryteachers.wikispaces.com/USII.12

Imagine, for example, an elementary, middle, or high school class studying the Great Depression and the New Deal of the 1930s—a required U.S. curriculum standard in every state. To learn about this historical period, students and teachers examine the Stock Market Crash and changing roles of federal agencies in the context of a New Deal philosophy in which the "forces of government should be marshaled to improve the conditions for the greatest number of Americans, with particular emphasis on the excluded and disadvantaged" (Tanenhaus, 2009).

The Great Depression and New Deal page on the *resourcesforhistoryteachers* wiki is an example of how a wiki tech book can expand learning resources beyond that of digital or paper textbooks. That page includes the following resources:

- *Picturing the 1930s*, from the Smithsonian American Art Museum through which students can create their own online documentaries using artifacts and objects from the museum's collection.
- *Interactive Periodic Table of the New Deal*, from the Franklin D. Roosevelt Presidential Library and Museum that explores the different federal agencies that were created to respond to the Depression.
- A lesson from the National Endowment for the Humanities on African Americans and the New Deal's Civilian Conservation Corps.
- Materials on women's roles during the Depression and the New Deal from the Digital Library of America.
- Links to primary documents including President Franklin D. Roosevelt's 1944 State of the Union Address where he set forth his Economic Bill of Rights.

These five selections—just some of the materials found on the *Great Depression and the New Deal* wiki page—demonstrate how a wiki tech book can present a range of multimodal resources to engage students in history learning.

Page Example: Population

> Visit the *Population* page:
> https://teachinggeography.wikispaces.com/Population

Population is a core topic in the study of geography. For the Population page on *Teaching Geography*, resources were found to explain the distribution of the world's population and the challenges of population growth. Then to expand the study of this topic, material was added about Thomas Malthus and Charles Darwin; the role of pandemics in world history; and the social, political, economic, and ecological dynamics that cause civilizations to collapse and disappear.

In one-to-one laptop or tablet settings and in regular one or two computer classrooms, students and teachers can use wiki tech books as replacements for paper textbooks or as supplements to a district-purchased textbook series. In this latter approach, the textbook provides a chronological overview summarizing important developments within a time period. The wiki selections extend the information by providing interactive experiences that build and sustain student involvement with academic content. The learning experience is flipped away from teacher and textbook-centered presentations toward student exploration and investigation of online resources.

ONLINE ASSIGNMENTS FOR STUDENTS

Students respond to assignments at every grade level. There are end-of-chapter activities in most textbooks; teachers assign essay topics and ask questions on tests and quizzes; class discussions often include written responses about topics. Assignments with questions help students recall facts and consider new ideas; they engage students in analyzing, interpreting, and creating information; they serve as thought and conversation starters during large and small group class meetings (Rothstein & Santana, 2011).

Many teachers formulate assignments using Bloom's Taxonomy of learning objectives and thinking skills (Anderson & Krathwohl, 2001). The skills of "analyzing," "applying," "evaluating," and "creating" at the middle and the top of Bloom's framework encourage students to think critically, creatively, and transformatively. The bottom levels of the taxonomy ("remembering" and "understanding") are acquired by engaging in a wide range of thinking about academic topics.

Crafting assignments is particularly important in flipped learning because student responses to outside-of-class reading and viewing develop the ideas and information needed for in-class learning experiences. Factual questions help students recall names, dates, and definitions they need to know when participating in discussions and taking unit exams. Analytically based questions ask students to do more with information by analyzing data, applying concepts to everyday life, and creating new ways to solve problems.

Two wikis, for a college course in education and for an upper elementary or middle school literature class, offer examples of crafting assignments as part of flipped learning where students write responses based on the different levels of Bloom's Taxonomy.

Page Example: TEAMS-Tutoring in Schools

Visit the *TEAMS-Tutoring in Schools*:
https://teams-tutoringinschools.wikispaces.com/Home

In *Education 4971: Tutoring in Schools*, a three-credit course in the College of Education at the University of Massachusetts Amherst, college students write weekly responses to multimodal wiki pages as the outside-of-class component of a flipped learning model. The course is part of the TEAMS Tutoring Project where university undergraduate and graduate students provide academic tutoring to culturally and linguistically diverse youngsters in local elementary, middle, and high school classrooms and after-school programs. In addition to in-school tutoring and online learning, college students attend a weekly two and one-half hour in-person class that explores learning theories, tutoring, and teaching strategies, and the impacts of class, race, gender, identity, and technology in K–12 schools.

For many years, the on-campus component of the TEAMS tutoring course was organized as teacher-led discussions in the format of a college seminar. To flip the course, we used a wiki and student writing to restructure the outside-of-class component of the class. Before coming to class each week, college students access the course wiki to read, listen, watch, and interact with online resources for that week's topic. Students then write weekly reflection/analysis/discovery responses based on their outside-of-class assignments. During class time, they participate in small group learning activities related to course topics and in-school tutoring experiences. The combination of online reading and viewing, weekly writing, in-class learning activities, and outside-of-class tutoring makes this flipped learning approach memorable for students.

The TEAMS course's "Whose History/Whose Science" topic offers examples of posing questions using Bloom's thinking skills framework. The week's overall focus is for college tutors to consider that the ways history and science is taught in schools can impact the engagement, motivation, and achievement of the students they are tutoring. Tutors assess the importance of viewing history as story (his-stories and her-stories), science as inquiry, and how multicultural materials can interest diverse students in learning important curriculum topics.

Page Example: Whose History/Whose Science

Visit the TEAMS wiki *Whose History/Whose Science* page:
https://teams-tutoringinschools.wikispaces.com/Whose+History

The online assignment for "Whose History/Whose Science" week has three sections, each with questions for students to answer.

- The first section introduces the twentieth-century documentary photographer and political activist Milton Rogovin who was a target of the 1950s Red Scare. Rogovin's contribution as a chronicler of daily lives and struggles of ordinary Americans is not part of most history and humanities courses or curriculum. After viewing a slideshow of his pictures, listening to a video and a podcast interview with the photographer, and exploring the website *Humans of New York*, students are asked "How could you introduce Milton Rogovin to students in ways they would find interesting or intriguing by connecting their own lives with the people he photographed?"
- The second section shows word clouds from seven presidential State of the Union addresses. A word cloud pictorially displays the words used in a text, with the most used terms appearing in larger font sizes. Students are asked to list the ten largest words in each word cloud and then comment on how younger learners "might respond to seeing a speech in a word cloud before they read or hear the entire text."
- The third section asks students to locate at least two online multimodal resources that could be used in a lesson focusing on the contributions of women important in the fields of math, science, history, or literature. Online multimodal resources include videos, audio broadcasts, podcasts, pictures and images, interactive websites. And learning games, as well as text-based materials. Students are asked to describe each resource they located and how it can differentiate learning for younger students.

Page Example: Chain of Fire

Visit *Chain of Fire* page:
https://teachingresourcesforenglish.wikispaces.com/Chain+of+Fire

A multimodal wiki page for the young adult novel *Chain of Fire* by South African writer Beverley Naidoo presents an example of assigning questions using different thinking skills for upper elementary and middle school students to answer. Set in the era of racial apartheid in South Africa, the book tells the struggle of Naledi who, with the help of her friend Taolo, must decide whether to remain quiet to ensure safety for her family or speak out in opposition to the government's plans to move her community to new racially separate "homelands."

Accessing the wiki page, students write answers to questions before, during, and after reading the book, using different thinking skills within Bloom's Taxonomy:

- *For understanding*:
  - "What are sources of conflict on a global scale as well as within your community that cause people to stand up for what they believe in?"
  - "What obstacles do people face as they work toward a resolution for these problems?"
- *For applying and analyzing*:
  - "What issues are students your age talking about or fighting for, and what can students do to take action and make change happen?"
- *For evaluating*:
  - "How would you compare your personal experience fighting for a cause or working for a change to that of Nadeli and Taolo?"
- *For creating*:
  - "If you won a contest with a prize of $1,000,000, how would you use it to help you solve a problem you want to change?"

In both the college and upper elementary/middle school examples, asking students to use different thinking skills to answer questions creates engagement and interest while building a framework for in-class activities and discussions based on the topics of the course. Through their answers, students demonstrate their knowledge of academic content while also expressing their personal views about what that information means to them in terms of their own lives.

In course evaluations, college students and younger learners agree that they enjoy using multimodal materials posted on educational wikis, and they like writing answers to questions that ask about their own ideas and perspectives. They prefer not just reading a printed text, but being able to listen, view, and interact with resources that provide content in ways that build interest and focus attention. They value opportunities for reflection, analysis, and discovery that come from answering questions where they are asked to compare, contrast, evaluate, create, and connect ideas to their own lives.

There are three key strategies to using wikis and student assignments as part of the outside-of-class component of flipped learning. First, online wiki pages need to offer a variety of learning experiences. Variety builds and sustains interest since students are reading, listening, viewing, and doing different activities as part of every assignment.

Second, writing answers to questions posed up and down Bloom's Taxonomy lets students analyze online resources while gaining academic information. Students express their knowledge and ideas and then revisit and reconsider those comments as the course proceeds, and they gain new knowledge from their class activities and in-school tutoring. Third, written responses enable teachers to assess the extent to which students read, listen, or view a resource and understand its information, letting teachers plan more concretely how students will discuss academic content and share ideas with each other during in-class activities.

WIKIQUESTS AS A FLIPPED LEARNING ACTIVITY

WikiQuests are a flipped learning variation of WebQuests where students access web content and complete academic assignments (Maloy et al., 2016). In a WikiQuest, unlike a WebQuest, students visit only sites contained in a teacher or classroom wiki. While there is no guarantee that students will not go to off-topic sites, a WikiQuest has the advantage of sending students to one online location for all the parts of an assignment. Setting up the wiki so that links open in separate tabs further helps students to focus on the academic components of their online quests.

In 1995, Bernie Dodge of San Diego State University developed the first WebQuest with the support of Tom March of the San Diego Unified School District and teachers and students at the Thatcher School. He defined a WebQuest as an "inquiry-oriented lesson format in which most or all of the information that learners work with comes from the web" (Dodge, 1995). His goal was for teachers to have broad flexibility in creating lessons based on digital content.

Here is one WikiQuest examples: (1) a Vietnam War WikiQuest, where students evaluate different historical resources in preparation for an in-class jigsaw activity where individuals share what they learned online in small groups.

Page Example: A Vietnam War WikiQuest

Visit *Vietnam War WikiQuest* page:
http://resourcesforhistoryteachers.wikispaces.com/Vietnam+War+Wikiquest

For the Vietnam War WikiQuest, students read and view text, audio, video, speeches, interviews, photos, and court case documents related to the American role in the conflict. The resources are connected to a U.S. history standard, "Explain the causes, course, and consequences of the Vietnam War and summarize the diplomatic and military policies of Presidents Eisenhower, Kennedy, Johnson, and Nixon." To provide a multimodal and multicultural learning experience, resources were arranged in four sections: Background, Primary Sources, Multimedia Sources, and Multicultural Sources.

- **Background and Overview**

  - *Vietnam and Southeast Asia History* from Columbia University's Asia for Educators website
  - *Battlefield Vietnam: A Brief History* from PBS
  - *Teaching the "American War": Looking at the War in Vietnam through Vietnamese Eyes* from the website, "Primary Source"

- **Primary Sources**

  - *Text of the Vietnamese Declaration of Independence*, 1945
  - *Vietnam War Causalities by Home of Record* from the Virtual Wall at the Vietnam Veterans Memorial
  - President Lyndon B. Johnson's Message to Congress, August 5, 1964
  - President Lyndon B. Johnson's 1968 speech *"Peace in Vietnam and Southeast Asia"* in which he announced he would not seek reelection as president
  - Reverend Martin Luther King, Jr.'s 1967 speech, *"Beyond Vietnam: A Time to Break the Silence"* in which he declared his opposition to the war
  - *Vietnam: An Anti-War Comic Book* by the civil rights activist Julian Bond

- **Multimedia Sources**

  - *Vietnam: A Television History* from PBS (selections from Episode 1)
  - *The War in Vietnam: A Story in Photographs* from the National Archives with documentary pictures of the war shot by military photographers between 1962 and 1975
  - *The Vietnam War*, a video from Kahn Academy
  - A podcast critiquing the Pentagon Vietnam War memorial website by historian Nick Turse

- **Multicultural Sources**

  - Documents and court case material related to *Clay v. United States*, the 1971 Supreme Court case arising from Muhammad Ali's (Cassius Clay) appeal of his 1967 conviction for refusing to report for military induction
  - *Spotlight on African Americans* from the Vietnam Center and Archive, Texas Tech University

- Excerpts of first-person interviews from *Patriots: The Vietnam War Remembered from All Sides* by historian Christian Appy—available as part of the "Look Inside" the book feature on Amazon.com

Students were asked to explore different sources from each section of the page and respond in writing to the following questions: Who produced the source? When was it produced? What is the perspective of the source? Is there more than one perspective? What are the main points of the source? Is the source trustworthy? How does the source relate to class notes, discussions and readings? Using facts, observations and background knowledge, what is the essential question answered by the source?

The Vietnam War WikiQuest uses student research and writing to flip the classroom learning experience. By composing responses to questions and then presenting ideas to peers in class, students steer their own learning by acting as researchers of academic content. They become aware of different types of online resources and then use their writing to analyze the materials' historical importance.

STUDENTS CONTRIBUTING TO WIKI PAGES

Students making substantive contributions to wiki pages are another way to generate flipped learning experiences in history and humanities classes. Contributing means students add to and revise material on pages, extending, changing, and clarifying information from earlier page builders. Students can also post their own creative and analytical writing, taking pages in new directions and opening new topics for exploration. As readers, writers, and page contributors, students become members of "communities of inquiry around topics" through which they "move toward a more complete set of understandings about people and events" (Cummings & Barton, 2008).

Students contribute to educational wikis, individually or as members of small composing and editing teams. They start a new page, shaping its look and structure by posting content. Alternately, students can post specific types of resources on existing pages by adding links to primary source documents, film and video resources, timelines, and websites about influential people in history. They serve as ongoing page curators—locating typos, correcting factual inaccuracies, and removing and replacing broken links.

By acting as page reviewers, editors, contributors, and designers, students practice and gain the knowledge and skills of digital research and information literacy. As they access, assess, and post resources, students become creators of online information, enlarging the scope of flipped learning by doing the outside-of-class work that can be the foundation for in-class activities and discussions. Progressive Wiki Page Building and Creative Story Writing are two examples of students becoming wiki page contributors.

Progressive Wiki Page Building

Progressive wiki page building is a variation of a creative writing activity known as a "progressive story" (Sheridan, 2012). In a progressive story, a teacher or student begins a story by posting an interest-building opening sentence ("Without warning, an alien spaceship appeared on the horizon") or describing the arrival of an unusual character ("The guest swept into the room like a tornado"). Subsequent writers then take turns adding sentences and paragraphs so the story unfolds from the collaborative and imaginative contributions of multiple authors.

The writers of a progressive wiki page do not have to be in face-to-face communication with one another. Rather, each writer spontaneously responds to what previous authors have written, letting their ideas and responses shape the plot, setting, characters, and resolution of the story.

A similar progressive writing process can happen with wiki pages. Teachers start a page, addressing a topic while leaving multiple subtopics for students to explore based on their research. For example, a teacher might post information about how to become an American on a page devoted the rights and responsibilities of citizens, but leave sections for students to research on the experiences of European immigrants, African Americans, Native Americans, and Asian and Mexican immigrants. Labor strikes and peasant revolts, Supreme Court decisions on voting rights, pandemics in world history, and the roles of women in math, science, and technology are other examples of topics explored through pages that teachers start and students continue building.

In progressive wiki page building, students read a page and add text, links, images, charts, and other resources to what the teacher and other students have previously posted. A teacher, or a teacher and students acting as editors and webmasters, then review what has been posted, removing inaccurate or outdated material. The pages grow progressively over time. Here are two examples: high school students adding to the Key Concept pages for Advanced Placement (AP) World History and creative writing by students during a literature study of Grimm's Fairy Tales.

Page Example: AP Key Concept Pages

> Visit the *AP World History* Main Page at https://resourcesforhisto
> ryteachers.wikispaces.com/AP+World+History

Each AP World History Key Concept page covers one of six time periods, following a format set by the College Board (2011) for national AP World History exam. Each page has deals with different countries and regions of the world, so students can choose a region of the world and add material to a page for that region and time period. The pages already have material posted by previous contributors, namely public school AP world history teachers and college students from our university's History Teacher Education Program.

Working from already existing pages, the high school students could act like progressive storywriters—reading what others had written and then adding new information based on their knowledge and interest, as in the following examples.

- For AP Key Concept 5.2: Imperialism and Nation- State Formation, the students posted short written statements on European military technology and tactics, the definition of nationalism, the characteristics of European imperialism, examples of native resistance, and Dutch control of Indonesia.
- For AP Key Concept 5.4: Global Migration, previous contributors had posted material on the Chinese Exclusion Acts that limited Chinese immigration to the United States. Building on the theme of how non-white immigrants faced ethnic and racial prejudice when they came to a new country, one student posted material on the White Australia Policy, an effort begun in the 1850s to exclude Asians (first Chinese and then Japanese) from that country. A classmate then added a link to YouTube video about the White Australia Policy.
- For AP Key Concept 6.3: New Conceptualizations of Global Economy, Society and Culture in the twentieth century, the students added references about women's suffrage movements around the world, the Space Race, the American Civil Rights Movement, the Olympics, and government responses to economic challenges including Franklin Roosevelt and the New Deal in the United States, Five-Year Plans in the Soviet Union under Joseph Stalin, and the Great Leap Forward in China under Mao Zedong.

On some pages, the students built on each other's contributions as well as the postings of earlier writers. On the Key Concept 6.3 page, one student added the following reference about the Great Leap Forward in China:

- Great Leap Forward (1958–1961). This plan developed agriculture and industry which Mao believed were needed to feed off each other. To allow for this, China was reformed into a series of communes.

Building on that student's entry, a second student added more information about the Great Leap Forward as well as background on Stalin's Five Year Plans:

- Mao Zedong attempted to remove all landlords and create an agrarian society. He attempted to modernize Chinese culture as well. Joseph Stalin's 5-year plan (1928). There was development of machines, steel, and transportation. Stalin starved the farmers in Europe's Bread Basket and sent all food to factory workers. Farmers had to buy from black markets to survive.

While these entries, like most of the postings by the students in the class, were relatively short in length, they represent original contributions to Key Concept pages. The students had to understand each Key Concept academically in order to post substantive, historically based information. In so doing, the students created a foundation on which more resources could be added in progressive story fashion. As editors, we subsequently posted a link to a website featuring Great Leap Forward propaganda posters to extend the students' China contributions.

Page Example: Grimm's Fairy Tales

Visit *Grimm's Fairy Tales* Page:
https://teachingresourcesforenglish.wikispaces.com/Grimm%27s+Fairy+Tales

CREATIVE STORY WRITING

Children's and Household Tales by Jacob and Wilhelm Grimm, known today as Grimm's Fairy Tales, were first published in 1812. The tales are among the most widely known collections of European folklore. Librarians and philological scholars, the Brothers Grimm gathered the tales from the oral tradition of German society as a way to record and preserve the culture. The first collection of the tales, noted comparative literature professor Jack Zipes (2015), was "brusque, blunt, absurd, comical, and tragic." Rather than benign fairy tales for children to read, many were "stark narratives about the brutal living conditions in the nineteenth century" (Zipes, 2015).

Between 1812 and 1857, the Brothers revised their story collection extensively to fit the interests of readers. They added new tales, embellished others, and omitted some entirely. In some cases, overtly sexual references and graphic violence were removed in the later tales. By the twentieth century, Grimm's stories "would become the most famous collection of folk and fairy tales in the western world" (Zipes, 2015).

As part of a combined history/humanities unit at one Massachusetts school, middle school students study the Grimm's tales in contrast to their modern-day adaptations as Disney movies and cartoons as well as related commercial products. Walt Disney began retelling traditional folktales in 1922 and dozens of tales from the Brothers Grimm, Hans Christian Anderson, Charles Perrault, Aesop, and other sources now have versions on film. Disney's entertainment approach has even resulted in a new word for the dictionary—disneyfy or disneyfied, meaning to change an original, often unsettling or distributing image or story into something simplified, wholesome, and nonthreatening.

Utilizing a flipped learning approach, teacher Sinead Meaney designed her Grimm's Fairy Tale unit so students would go to the *Teaching Resources for English* wiki to learn about the history and style of the tales, and then, using that knowledge, create their own version of a tale to post on the site. She built individual wiki pages for several of the most well-known tales: Cinderella, Hansel and Gretel, Rapunzel, Little Red Riding Hood, Snow White, Rumpelstiltskin, and The Hare and the Hedgehog.

Each page contained links to the original text of the story, an audio retelling, a video version, Disney connections, and instructional lesson plans along with images from Wikimedia Commons depicting key themes from the stories. When available, interesting sidelights were included such as how the Cinderella story is told differently in countries and cultures around the world; how Snow White may have been based on real-life stories from European society; how the 1812 and 1857 versions of Rapunzel differ in tone and plot; or how students can design their own online opera for Hansel and Gretel.

After reviewing the pages and discussing the genre of folktales in class, students were invited, individually or in pairs, to complete one of the following creative writing and drawing projects: (1) Disneyfy a Grimm's tale by removing its harsh features and replacing them with a romanticized version like those in Disney cartoons and movies; (2) create a fractured fairy tale that keeps elements of the original tale, but changes the plot, characters, setting and story resolution in new, often humorous ways; and (3) produce an original digital fairy tale story using iMovie or GreenScreen or making an audio recording of the story to accompany student-drawn illustrations. Other project choices included constructing a visual presentation that compares and contrasts a Grimm Brothers' story with a Disney version of the same tale or constructing a new ending to an old tale and performing it in class.

Enthusiastically, the students chose their projects and created new versions of old stories, including, "The Little Red Riding Hood as Told by The Wolf," "The Little Mermaid in a Fish Tank," "Hans the Happy Hedgehog," and "Snow Brown and the 7 Hipsters." Two girls collaborated on a version entitled "The Juniper Tree Disneyfied." Two boys worked together to code a Cinderella game while other two girls created "Cinder Smella: A Twist on the Disney Tale." A group of three students posted a QuickTime video story entitled "Snow Queen in Hawaii."

The wiki provided motivation and resources for the students. "They liked being able to look up information independently from the wiki," said the teacher who added that students were ecstatic about having their projects featured on one of the Grimm's Tales wiki pages. Next year, the teacher said, "I'd like to have them spending more time working on the pages as it's something they were interested it. I learned that they want to be more a part of adding on to it [the wiki] and to blow me away with how creative and capable they are!"

Progressive page building and the writing of new version of old tales demonstrate how wikis can continue to grow and expand when students are active contributors of online content. Three factors propel students to contribute to wikis: (1) students have a strong sense of personal ownership of what they write; (2) students enjoy reading and viewing what other students have contributed; and (3) students are amazed and energized by the reality that people around the world can read and view their work. Once launched, teachers can continue progressive page building and fairy tale writing projects year-to-year as new groups of students add their work to wiki pages. Teacher- and student-made wikis expand as they grow to be an archive of creative contributions, each year's additions giving more depth and dimension to history and humanities learning.

References

ALA Digital Literacy Taskforce. (2013, January). *Digital literacy, libraries, and public policy*. Retrieved from American Library Association website: http://www.districtdispatch.org/wp-content/uploads/2013/01/2012_OITP_digilitreport_1_22_13.pdf

Anderson, L. W., & Krathwohl, D. R. (Eds.). (2001). *A taxonomy for learning, teaching, and assessing: A revision of Bloom's Taxonomy of educational objectives*. New York: Longman.

Association of College & Research Libraries. (2000). *Information literacy competency standards for higher education*. Retrieved from http://www.ala.org/acrl/standards/informationliteracycompetency#ildef

Austin, H. M., & Thompson, K. (2014). *Examining the evidence: Seven strategies for teaching with primary sources*. North Mankato, MN: Capstone Classroom.

Bain, D. H. (2000). *Empire express: Building the first transcontinental railroad*. New York: Vintage.

Barbey, S. (2009, October 26). More than an encyclopedia. [Web log post]. Retrieved from http://www.iwawaterwiki.org/xwiki/bin/view/About/WebHome

Barnes & Noble College. (2016). *Getting to know Gen Z: Exploring middle and high schoolers' expectations for higher education*. Retrieved from http://next.bncollege.com/wp-content/uploads/2015/10/Gen-Z-Research-Report-Final.pdf

Baron, N. S. (2015). *Words onscreen: The fate of reading in a digital world*. New York: Oxford University Press.

Bergmann, J., & Sams, A. (2012). *Flip your classroom: Reach every student in every class every day*. Arlington, VA: International Society for Technology in Education.

Bergmann, J., & Sams, A. (2014). *Flipped learning: Gateway to student engagement*. Arlington, VA: International Society for Technology in Education.

Bergmann, J., & Sams, A. (2015). *Flipped learning for elementary instruction*. Arlington, VA: International Society for Technology in Education.

Bigelow, B. (n.d.). Discovering Columbus: Re-reading the past. [Web log post]. Retrieved from http://zinnedproject.wpengine.netdna-cdn.com/wp-content/uploads/2009/11/discovering_columbus.pdf

Bigelow, B. (2008). *A people's history for the classroom*. Milwaukee: Rethinking Schools.

Binfield, K. (2015). *Writings of the Luddites*. Baltimore: Johns Hopkins University Press.

Blackboard. (2016). *How K-12 leaders are empowering personalized learning in America's schools*. Washington, D.C: Author.

Bronski, M. (2011). *A queer history of the United States*. Boston: Beacon Press.

Buchanan, T. C. (2004). *Black life on the Mississippi: Slaves, free blacks, and the western steamboat world*. Chapel Hill: University of North Carolina Press.

Burbules, N. C. (2001, Winter). Paradoxes of the Web: Dimensions of credibility. *Library Trends, 49*(3), 441–453.

Burbules, N. C., & Callister, T. A. Jr. (2000). *WatchIT: The risks and promise of information technologies for education*. Boulder, CO: Westview Press.

Calder, L. (2006, March). Uncoverage: Toward a signature pedagogy for the history survey. *Journal of American History*, 1358–1370.

California Department of Education. (2015). *Frequently asked questions: Senate bill 48*. Retrieved from http://www.cde.ca.gov/ci/cr/cf/senatebill48faq.asp

Carr, N. (2011). *The shallows: What the Internet is doing to our brains*. New York: W. W. Norton & Company.

Center for Digital Education & National School Boards Association. (2015). *Digital school districts survey*. Retrieved from http://www.centerdigitaled.com/awards/digital-districts/National-Survey-Recognizes-School-Districts-for-Innovative-Uses-of-Technology.html

Cherry, S. (2011, February 22). Don't believe everything you see on the Internet. *IEEE Spectrum*. Retrieved from http://spectrum.ieee.org/podcast/at-work/education/do-you-believe-this-headline

Clabough, J., Turner, T. N., Russell, W. B. III, & Waters, S. (2016). *Unpuzzling history through primary sources*. Charlotte, NC: Information Age Publishing, Inc.

Coiro, J. (2014, April 7). Teaching adolescents how to evaluate the quality of online information. *Edutopia*. Retrieved from http://www.edutopia.org/blog/evaluating-quality-of-online-info-julie-coiro

Coiro, J., Coscarelli, C., Maykel, C., & Forzani, E. (2015, November/December). Investigating criteria that seventh graders use to evaluate the quality of online information. *Journal of Adolescent & Adult Literacy, 59*(3), 287–297.

College Board. (2011, Fall). *AP world history course and exam description*. Retrieved from https://secure-media.collegeboard.org/digitalServices/pdf/ap/ap-world-history-course-and-exam-description.pdf

Collins, A., & Halverson, R. (2009). *Rethinking education in the age of technology: The digital revolution and schooling in America*. New York: Teachers College Press.

Collins, R. (2010). *Leadership in a wiki world. Leveraging collective knowledge to make the leap to extraordinary performance*. Indianapolis: Dog Ear Publishing.

Committee on Communications. (2006, December). Children, adolescents and advertising. *Pediatrics, 118*(6). Retrieved from http://pediatrics.aappublications.org/content/118/6/2563

Common Core State Standards Initiative. (2016). *Literacy in History/Social Studies, Science, & Technical Subjects*. Washington, D.C.: Council of Chief State School Officers and National Governors Association Center for Best Practices.

Common Sense Media. (2014, Spring). *Advertising to children and teens: Current practices.* San Francisco: Author.

Common Sense Media. (2015, November 3). Landmark report: U.S. teens use an average of nine hours of media per day, tweens use six hours. Retrieved from https://www.commonsensemedia.org/about-us/news/press-releases/landmark-report-us-teens-use-an-average-of-nine-hours-of-media-per-day#

Consortium for School Networking. (2015). *CoSN K-12 IT leadership survey report.* Retrieved from http://cosn.org/sites/default/files/pdf/CoSN_ITLdrship_Report_v4IKS_SL.pdf?sid=7307

Cooper, S. (2015, April 19). Teaching MS history: Themes or timelines? *MiddleWeb.* Retrieved from http://www.middleweb.com/21968/teaching-ms-history-themes-or-timelines/

Cuban, L. (1993). *How teachers taught: Constancy and change in American classrooms, 1890–1990.* New York: Teachers College Press.

Cuban, L. (2008). *Hugging the middle: How teachers teach in an era of testing and accountability.* New York: Teachers College Press.

Cuban, L. (2013). *Inside the black box of classroom practice: Change without reform in American education.* Cambridge, MA: Harvard Education Press.

Cuban, L. (2016). *Teaching history then and now: A story of stability and change.* Cambridge, MA: Harvard University Press.

Cummings, R. E., & Barton, M. (Eds.). (2008). *Wiki writing: Collaborative learning in the college classroom.* Ann Arbor: University of Michigan Press.

Darling-Hammond, L., Zielezinski, M., & Goldman, S. (2014, September). *Using technology to support at-risk students' learning.* Stanford, CA: Stanford Center for Opportunity Policy in Education. Retrieved from https://edpolicy.stanford.edu/sites/default/files/scope-pub-using-technology-report.pdf

Dever, M. T., Sorenson, B., & Broderick, J. (2005). Using picture books as a vehicle to teach young children about social justice. *Social Studies and the Young Learner, 18*(1), 18–21.

Dewey, J. (1943). *The child and the curriculum and the school and the society.* Chicago: University of Chicago Press.

Dewey, C. (2016, June 20). "The surprising reasons some college professors telling students to use Wikipedia for class." *The Washington Post.* Retrieved from https://www.washingtonpost.com/news/the-intersect/wp/2016/06/20/the-surprising-reason-some-college-professors-are-telling-students-to-use-wikipedia-for-class/?utm_term=.5c23cc490916

Dodge, B. (1995). Some thoughts about WebQuests. Retrieved from http://webquest.org/sdsu/about_webquests.html

Dunbar-Ortiz, R. (2014). *An indigenous peoples' history of the United States.* Roxanne. Boston: Beacon Press.

Eaklor, V. L. (2011). *Queer America: A people's GLBT history of the United States.* New York: New Press People's History.

Ebersbach, A., Glaser, M., Heigi, R., & Dueck, G. (2008). *Wiki: Web collaboration* (2nd ed.). Berlin: Springer.

Education Week. (2015). *Technology counts 2015: Learning the digital way.* Retrieved from http://www.edweek.org/ew/toc/2015/06/11/index.html?intc=EW-TC15-LNAV

Education Week. (2016). *Technology Counts 2016: Transforming the classroom.* Retrieved from http://www.edweek.org/ew/toc/2016/06/09/

Educause Learning Initiative. (2005, July). *7 things you should know about . . . wikis.* Retrieved from https://net.educause.edu/ir/library/pdf/ELI7004.pdf

Educause Learning Initiative. (2012, February). *7 things you should know about . . . flipped classrooms.* Retrieved from https://net.educause.edu/ir/library/pdf/eli7081.pdf

Edwards, S. A., & Maloy, R. W. (1992). *Kids have all the write stuff: Inspiring your child to put pencil to paper.* New York: Penguin Books.

Evans, S. (1997). *Born for liberty.* New York: The Free Press.

Fernandez-Armesto, F. (2007). *A global history of exploration.* New York: W. W. Norton, 2007.

Fillpot, E. (n.d.). Teaching with timelines. *Teachinghistory.org.* Retrieved from http://teachinghistory.org/digital-classroom/tech-for-teachers/24268

Flipped Learning Network. (2014, March 13). Flipped learning network unveils formal definition of flipped learning. Retrieved from http://flippedlearning.org/cms/lib07/VA01923112/Centricity/Domain/46/FLN_Definition_Release_FINAL.pdf

Foshay, R., & Bergeron, C. (2000). Web-based education: A reality check. *Tech Trends, 44*(5), 16–19.

Fraser, E. D., & Rimas, A. (2010). *Empires of food: Feast, famine and the rise and fall of civilizations.* New York: The Free Press.

Freeman, E., Schamel, W. B., & West, J. (1992, February). The fight for equal rights: A recruiting poster for Black soldiers in the Civil War. *Social Education 56*(2), 118–120. [Revised and updated in 1999 by Budge Weidman.]

Fuller, K. H. (1999). Lessons from the screen: Film and video in the classroom. *Perspectives on History.* Retrieved from https://www.historians.org/publications-and-directories/perspectives-on-history/april-1999/lessons-from-the-screen-film-and-video-in-the-classrooom

Galeano, E. (2013). *Children of the days: A calendar of human history.* New York: Nation Books.

Gartley, E. (2015, October 25). School is in: LGBT history is history. *GBLT News: Gay, Lesbian, Bisexual, and Transgender Round Table of the American Library Association.* Retrieved from https://resourcesforhistoryteachers.wikispaces.com/home

Gee, J. P. (2007). *What video games have to teach us about learning and literacy.* (Revised and updated edition). New York: St. Martin's Griffin.

Gee, J. P. (2013). *The anti-education era: Creating smarter students through digital learning.* New York: St. Martin's.

Gonzalez, J. (2011). *Harvest of empire: A history of Latinos in America.* New York: Penguin Books.

Greenfield, S. (2015). *Mind change: How digital technologies are leaving their mark on our brains.* New York: Random House.

Grigas, V. (2014, May 26). Happy birthday, Ward Cunningham, inventor of the wiki. *Wikimedia Blog.* Retrieved from http://blog.wikimedia.org/2014/05/26/happy-birthday-ward-cunningham-inventor-of-the-wiki/

Groenke, S. L., & Scherff, L. (2010). *Teaching YA Lit through differentiated instruction.* Urbana, IL: National Council of Teachers of English.

Guernsey, L., & Levine, M. H. (2015). *Tap, click, read: Growing readers in a world of screens*. San Francisco: Jossey-Bass.

Herold, B. (2015, June 10). Why Ed Tech is not transforming how teachers teach. *Technology Counts 2015: Learning the digital way*. Retrieved from http://www.edweek.org/ew/articles/2015/06/11/why-ed-tech-is-not-transforming-how.html

Houston, K. (2016). *The book: A cover-to-cover exploration of the most powerful object of our time*. New York: W. W. Norton & Company.

International Society for Technology in Education. (2016). ISTE Standards for Students. Retrieved from http://www.iste.org/standards/standards/for-students-2016

Jelen, J. (2011, February 21). Beyond butcher paper. *Teachinghistory.org*. Retrieved from http://teachinghistory.org/nhec-blog/24425

Johnson, D. K. (2004). *The lavender scare: The Cold War persecution of gays and lesbians in the federal government*. Chicago: University of Chicago Press.

Johnson, K. (2011, February 17). Researching patents of African American inventors. *New York Public Library*. Retrieved from http://www.nypl.org/blog/2011/02/17/researching-patents-african-american-inventors

Kahne, J., & Bowyer, B. (2016, November 4). Educating for democracy in a partisan age: Confronting the challenge of motivated reasoning and misinformation. *American Educational Research Journal*. Retrieved from http://ypp.dmlcentral.net/publications/313

Kawakita, C. (2017). A collaboration of sites and sounds: Using wikis to catalog protest songs. *ReadWriteThink*. Urbana, IL: National Council of Teachers of English. Retrieved from http://www.readwritethink.org/classroom-resources/lesson-plans/collaboration-sites-sounds-using-979.html

Kohl, H. (1991). The politics of children's literature. The story of Rosa Parks and the Montgomery Bus Boycott. *The Journal of Education, 173*(1), 35–50.

Lakwete, A. (2003). *Inventing the cotton gin: Machine and myth in antebellum America*. Baltimore: The Johns Hopkins University Press.

LaRoche, I. S. (2015). *Expanding democracy in classrooms: History teacher candidates' perceptions of student feedback as a democratic practice* (Doctoral dissertation). Retrieved from http://umass.worldcat.org.silk.library.umass.edu/title/expanding-democracy-in-classrooms-history-teacher-candidates-perceptions-of-student-feedback-as-a-democratic-teaching-practice/oclc/930710005&referer=brief_results

Laufenberg, D. (2011, April 20). The pitfalls of chronology. *Teachinghistory.org*. Retrieved from http://teachinghistory.org/nhec-blog/24585

Lesh, B. A. (2011). *Why won't you just tell us the answer? Teaching historical thinking grades 7–12*. Portland, ME: Stenhouse.

Levathes, L. (1997). *When China ruled the seas: The treasure fleet of the dragon throne, 1405–1433*. New York: Oxford University Press.

Lienhard, J. H. (1988). Episode 124: Black inventors. *Engines of Our Ingenuity*. University of Houston. Retrieved from http://www.uh.edu/engines/epi127.htm

Lih, A. (2009). *The Wikipedia revolution: How a bunch of nobodies created the world's greatest encyclopedia*. New York: Hyperion.

Loewen, J. W. (2007). *Lies my teacher told me: Everything your American history textbook got wrong*. New York: The New Press.

References

Maloy, R. W., Greene, J., Malinowski, A., Emery, J., & Curtin, K. (2016, Fall). Wiki-quests, microblogging and personal response systems in the history classroom. *Teaching History: A Journal of Methods, XLI*(2), 84–98.

Maloy, R. W., & LaRoche, I. S. (2015). *We the students and teachers: Teaching democratically in the history and social studies classroom*. Albany: State University of New York Press.

Maloy, R. W., Poirier, M., Smith, H. K., & Edwards, S. A. (2010, November). The making of a standards wiki. *The History Teacher, 44*(1), 67–81.

Maloy, R. W., Verock, R. E., Edwards, S. A., & Woolf, B. P. (2017). *Transforming learning with new technologies*. (Third edition). Boston: Pearson.

Mann, C. C. (2005). *1491: New revelations of the Americas before Columbus*. New York: Knopf.

Massachusetts Department of Education. (2003). *Massachusetts history and social science curriculum framework*. Malden, MA: Author.

Mayer, R. E. (2009). *Multimedia learning* (2nd ed.). New York: Cambridge University Press.

Mayer, R. E. & Moreno, R. (2003). Nine ways to reduce cognitive load in multimedia learning. *Educational Psychologist, 38*(1), 43–52.

McCall, J. (2011). Jeremiah McCall on using simulation games in the history classroom. *TeachingHistory.org*. Retrieved from http://teachinghistory.org/nhec-blog/25117

McCormick, T. M., & Hubbard, J. (2011, Spring). Every picture tells a story: A study of teaching methods using historical photographs with elementary students. *Journal of Social Studies Research, 35*(1), 80–94.

McGonigal, J. (2011). *Reality is broken: Why games make us better and how they can change the world*. New York: Penguin Press.

McNeill, W. H. (1985). Why study history? *American Historical Association*. Retrieved from, https://www.historians.org/about-aha-and-membership/aha-history-and-archives/archives/why-study-history-(1985)

McNeill, W. H. (1998). *Plagues and peoples*. New York: Random House.

Mehta, I. (2015, July 14). "Breadth and depth: Can we have it both ways?" *Education Week*. Retrieved from http://blogs.edweek.org/edweek/learning_deeply/2015/07/breadth_and_depth_can_we_have_it_both_ways.html

Miller, M. D. (2014). *Minds online: Teaching effectively with technology*. Cambridge, MA: Harvard University Press.

Minnesota Department of Education. (2013). *Minnesota K-12 academic standards: Social studies, 2011*. Retrieved from http://www.mcss.org/Resources/Documents/2011%20Social%20Studies%20Standards.pdf

National Council for the Social Studies. (2013). *The college, career, and civic life (C3) framework for social studies state standards: Guidance for enhancing the rigor of K-12 civics, economics, geography, and history*. Silver Spring, MD: NCSS.

National History Education Clearinghouse. (n.d.). *Opening up the textbook*. Retrieved from http://teachinghistory.org/best-practices/teaching-with-textbooks/19438

National Research Council. (2000). How people learn: Brain, mind, experience, and school: Expanded edition. Washington, DC: The National Academies Press. https://doi.org/10.17226/9853.

National Women's History Museum. (2007). *A history of women in industry.* Retrieved from http://archive.is/d6i9B

The *New York Times* Editorial Board. (2016, November 20). The digital virus called fake news. *New York Times Sunday Review*, 10.

Notari, M., Reynolds, R., Chu, S. K. W., & Honegger, B. D. (2016). *The wiki way of learning: Creating learning experiences using collaborative web pages.* Chicago: American Library Association.

Noveck, B. S. (2010). *Wiki government: How technology can make government better, democracy stronger, and citizens more powerful.* Washington, D.C.: Brookings Institution Press.

OECD. (2015). *Students, computers and learning: Making the connection.* PISA: OECD Publishing.

Ofcom. (2015, November). *Children and parents: Media and attitudes report.* Retrieved from http://stakeholders.ofcom.org.uk/binaries/research/media-literacy/children-parents-nov-15/childrens_parents_nov2015.pdf

O'Hara, S., & Pritchard, R. (2014). What is the impact of technology on learning? *Education.com.* Retrieved from http://www.education.com/reference/article/what-impact-technology-learning/

Papert, S. (1980). *Mindstorms: Children, computers, and powerful ideas* (2nd ed.). Cambridge, MA: Perseus Publishing.

Papert, S. (1993). *The children's machine: Rethinking school in the age of the computer.* New York: Basic Books.

Papert, S. (1996). *The connected family: Bridging the digital generation gap.* Atlanta: Longstreet Press.

Perrin, A. (2016a, November 23). *Who doesn't read books in America.* Pew Research Center. Retrieved from http://www.pewresearch.org/fact-tank/2016/11/23/who-doesnt-read-books-in-america/

Perrin, A. (2016b, September 1). *Book reading 2016.* Pew Research Center. Retrieved from http://www.pewinternet.org/2016/09/01/book-reading-2016/

Pomerance, L., Greenberg, J., & Walsh, K. (2015, January). *Learning about learning: What every new teacher needs to know.* Washington, D.C.: National Council on Teacher Quality.

Pomeranz, K., & Topik, S. (2005). *The world that trade created: Society, culture and the world economy, 1400—the present* (2nd ed.). New York: M.E. Sharpe.

Prensky, M. R. (2010). *Teaching digital natives: Partnering for real learning.* Thousand Oaks, CA: Corwin.

Pressey, B. (2013). *Comparative analysis of national teacher surveys.* New York: The Joan Ganz Cooney Center at Sesame Workshop.

Project Tomorrow. (2014). *The new digital learning playbook: Understanding the spectrum of students' activities and aspirations.* Retrieved from http://www.tomorrow.org/speakup/pdfs/SU13StudentsReport.pdf

Project Tomorrow. (2016). *From print to pixel: The role of videos, games, animations and simulations within K-12 education.* Retrieved from http://www.tomorrow.org/speakup/SU15AnnualReport.html

Purcell, K., Heaps, A., Buchanan, J., & Friedrich, L. (2013, February 28). *How teachers are using technology at home and their classrooms.* Pew Research Center.

Retrieved from http://www.pewinternet.org/2013/02/28/how-teachers-are-using-technology-at-home-and-in-their-classrooms/

Purcell, K., Rainie, L., Heaps, A., Buchanan, J., Friedrich, L., Jacklin, A., Chen, C., & Zickuhr, K. (2012, November 1). *How teens do research in the digital world*. Pew Research Center. Retrieved from www.pewinternet.org/2012/11/01/how-teens-do-research-in-the-digital-world/

Rainie, L., & Perrin, A. (2015, October 19). *Slightly fewer Americans are reading print books, new survey finds*. Pew Research Center. Retrieved from http://www.pewresearch.org/fact-tank/2015/10/19/slightly-fewer-americans-are-reading-print-books-new-survey-finds/

Rebora, A. (2016, June 6). Teachers still struggling to use technology to transform instruction, survey says. *Technology Counts 2016: Transforming the Classroom*. Retrieved from http://www.edweek.org/ew/articles/2016/06/09/teachers-still-struggling-to-use-tech-to.html?intc=EW-TC16-TOC

Reich, J., Murnane, R., & Willett, J. (2012). The state of wiki usage in U.S. K-12 schools: Leveraging Web 2.0 data warehouses to assess quality and equity in online learning environments. *Educational Researcher, 41*(1), 7–15.

Reynolds, J. C., Jr. (1976, January). American textbooks: The first 200 years. *Educational Leadership*. Retrieved from http://www.ascd.org/ASCD/pdf/journals/ed_lead/el_197601_reynolds.pdf

Richardson, W. (2010). *Blogs, wikis, podcasts and other powerful web tools for classrooms*. Thousand Oaks, CA: Corwin Press.

Ritchel, M. (2012, November 1). Technology is changing how students learn, teachers say. *New York Times*. Retrieved from http://www.nytimes.com/2012/11/01/education/technology-is-changing-how-students-learn-teachers-say.html?pagewanted=1&hpw&_r=0

Roberts, M. (2012). Why should we have all the fun? Encouraging colleagues to read YA novels across the curriculum. *English Journal, 102*(1), 92–95.

Roberts, S. (2006, September 14). Story of the first through Ellis Island is rewritten. *New York Times*. Retrieved from http://www.nytimes.com/2006/09/14/nyregion/14annie.html

Robertson, L. (2014, November 19). That chain e-mail your friend sent you is likely bogus. Seriously. *FactCheck.org*. Retrieved from http://www.factcheck.org/2008/03/that-chain-e-mail-your-friend-sent-to-you-is-likely-bogus-seriously/

Robertson, L., & Kiely, E. (2016, November 18). How to spot fake news. *FactCheck.org*. Retrieved from http://www.factcheck.org/2016/11/how-to-spot-fake-news/

Romesburg, D., Rupp, L. J., & Donahue, D. M. (2014). *Making the framework FAIR: California history-social science framework proposed LGBT revisions related to the FAIR Education Act*. San Francisco, CA: Committee on Lesbian, Gay, Bisexual, and Transgender History.

Rothstein, D., & Santana, L. (2011). *Make just one change: Teach students to ask their own questions*. Cambridge, MA: Harvard Education Press.

Sanchez, A. (2016, June 14). *What happened to the Civil Rights Movement after 1965? Don't ask your textbook*. Zinn Education Project. Retrieved from http://zinnedproject.org/2016/06/civil-rights-movement-after-1965-not-in-textbooks/

Schaffhauser, D., & Nagel, D. (2016, September). Teaching with tech: A love (and hate) story. *The Journal, 43*(5), 6–15.

Schleicher, A. (2015, September). School technology struggles to make an impact. *BBC News*. Retrieved from http://www.bbc.com/news/business-34174795

Schons, M. (2011, January 21). African-American inventors I. *National Geographic Society*. Retrieved from http://nationalgeographic.org/news/african-american-inventors-18th-century/

Schrock, K. (2015). The 5W's of web site evaluation. *Schrockguide.net*. Retrieved from http://www.schrockguide.net/uploads/3/9/2/2/392267/5ws.pdf

Seo, K. (Ed.). (2013). *Using social media effectively in the classroom: Blogs, wikis, twitter, and more*. New York: Routledge.

Shank, J. D. (2014). *Interactive open educational resources: A guide to finding, choosing and using what's out there to transform college teaching*. San Francisco: Jossey-Bass.

Shaw, S. (n.d.). Beyond biography: Teaching student historians to analyze and evaluate historical figures. *100 Leaders in World History*. Retrieved from http://100leaders.org/classroom-resources

Sheridan, B. J. (2012, February 6). Kinders collaborate & create progressive story using wiki & VoiceThread. Exploring digital media in education. Retrieved from https://www.coetail.com/bsheridan/2012/02/06/kinders-create-progressive-story-using-wiki-voicethread/

Sipress, J. M., & Voelker, D. J. (2011, March). The end of the history survey course: The rise and fall of the coverage model. *The Journal of American History, 97*(4) 1050–1066.

Skiena, S., & Ward, C. (2013). *Who's bigger: Where historical figures really rank*. New York: Cambridge University Press.

South Carolina Department of Education. (2012, June 18). *Support documents and resources: United States history and the Constitution*. Retrieved from http://ed.sc. gov/scdoe/assets/file/agency/ccr/Standards-Learning/documents/USHistorySupportDocuments.pdf

Southern Poverty Law Center Teaching Tolerance Project. (2012, March). *Teaching the movement: The state standards we deserve*. Retrieved from https://www.splcenter.org/sites/default/files/d6_legacy_files/downloads/publication/Teaching_the_Movement_2_3.pdf

Southern Poverty Law Center Teaching Tolerance Project. (2014, March). *Teaching the movement 2014: The state of civil rights education in the United States*. Retrieved from http://www.tolerance.org/TTM2014

Speaking of Tomorrow. (2016, August 31). *How we're using social media in and out of school*. Message posted to http://blog.tomorrow.org/index.php/2016/08/31/students-teachers-use-of-social-media/

Staley, D. J. (2013). *Computers, visualization and history: How new technology will transform our understanding of the past*. New York: Routledge.

The State Education Department and The University of the State of New York. (2015, January). *New York State grades 9–12 social studies framework: Revised*. Retrieved from https://www.engageny.org/resource/new-york-state-k-12-social-studies-framework

Symcox, L. (1991). *Introduction: Three worlds meet—The Columbian Encounter and its legacy*. Los Angeles: National Center for History in the Schools, UCLA Department of History

Takaki, R. (2008). *A different mirror: A history of multicultural America*. Boston: Little, Brown and Company.

Tanenhaus, S. (2009, August 30). The roar of the liberal. *New York Times*. Retrieved from http://query.nytimes.com/gst/fullpage.html?res=9903E4D8133EF933A0575BC0A96F9C8B63&pagewanted=all

Teresi, D. (2002). *Lost discoveries: The ancient roots of modern science—from the Babylonians to the Maya*. New York: Simon & Schuster.

Texas Freedom Network Education Fund. (2014, September). *Writing to the standards: Reviews of proposed social studies textbooks for Texas public schools—Executive summary*. Retrieved from http://www.tfn.org/site/DocServer/FINAL_executivesummary.pdf?docID=4625

Theoharis, J. (2014). *The rebellious life of Mrs. Rosa Parks*. Boston: Beacon Press.

To the Best of Our Knowledge. (2011). Living democracy: Transcript for Ward Cunningham on "The Wiki Way."

Turner, J. M. (2008, February 20). *African American technological contributions: Past, present, and future*. Black History Colloquium at the Johns Hopkins University Applied Physics Laboratory. Retrieved from http://www.nist.gov/director/speeches/turner_022008.cfm

VanSledright, B. A. (1997, January). Can more be less? The depth-breath dilemma in teaching American history. *Social Education, 61*(1), 38–47.

VanSledright, B. A. (2011). *The challenge of rethinking history education: On practices, theories, and policy*. New York: Routledge.

Venners, B. (2003, October 20). *Exploring with wiki: A conversation with Ward Cunningham, Part 1*. Retrieved from http://www.artima.com/intv/wiki.html

Viviano, F. (2005, July). China's great Amanda. *National Geographic*. Retrieved from http://ngm.nationalgeographic.com/ngm/0507/feature2/

Wiggins, G. J., & McTighe, J. (2005). *Understanding by design*. Alexandria, VA: Association for Supervision and Curriculum Development.

WikiEducator. (2010, October 29). *Defining OER*. Retrieved from http://wikieducator.org/Educators_care/Defining_OER

Wilson, M. (1954). *Science and invention: A pictorial history*. New York: Simon & Schuster.

Wineburg, S. (2007, June 5). Opening up the textbook and offering students a 'second voice'. *Education Week, 26*(30), 28–29.

Wineburg, S., Breakstone, J., McGrew, S., & Ortega, T. (2016, November). *Executive summary: Evaluating information—The cornerstone of civic online reasoning*. Stanford History Education Group, 1–27. Retrieved from https://sheg.stanford.edu/upload/V3LessonPlans/Executive%20Summary%2011.21.16.pdf

Wineburg, S., Martin, D., & Monte-Sano, C. (2013). *Reading like an historian: Teaching literacy in middle and high school history classrooms*. New York: Teachers College Press.

Wineburg, S., & Monte-Sano, C. (2008, March). "Famous Americans": The changing pantheon of American heroes. *The Journal of American History, 94*(4), 1186–1202.

Wolf, K. (1994, May). Teaching history the old fashioned way—through biography. *Perspectives on History: The Newsletter of the American Historical Association.* Retrieved from https://www.historians.org/publications-and-directories/perspectives-on-history/may-1994/teaching-history-the-old-fashioned-way-through-biography

Zheng, B., Warschauer, M., Lin, C.-H., & Chang, C. (2016). Learning in one-to-one laptop environments: A meta-analysis and research synthesis. *Review of Educational Research, XX*(X), 1–33.

Zickuhr, K., & Rainie, L. (2014, September 10). *Younger Americans reading habits and technology use.* Pew Research Center. Retrieved from http://www.pewinternet.org/2014/09/10/younger-americans-reading-habits-and-technology-use/

Zinn, H. (2015). *A people's history of the United States: 1492-present* (Reissue edition). New York: Harper Perennial.

Zinn, H., & Arnove, A. (2009). *Voices of a people's history of the United States.* New York: Seven Stories Press.

Zinn Education Project. (2013, July 17). *Former Indiana Gov. Mitch Daniels sought to ban Howard Zinn in public schools.* Retrieved from http://zinnedproject.org/2013/07/mitch-daniels/

Zinn Education Project. (2016). *About the Zinn Education Project.* Retrieved from http://zinnedproject.org/about/

Zipes, J. (2015, March/April). How the Grimm brothers saved the fairy tale. *Humanities, 36*(2). Retrieved from http://www.neh.gov/humanities/2015/marchapril/feature/how-the-grimm-brothers-saved-the-fairy-tale

Index

Note: Book titles, websites, and page numbers for wiki pages are *italicized*.

About the Authors

Robert W. Maloy is a senior lecturer in the College of Education, University of Massachusetts Amherst where he coordinates the history and political science teacher license program. He is coauthor of seven books including *Transforming Learning with New Technologies* and *We, The Students and Teachers: Teaching Democratically in the History and Social Studies Classroom*.

Allison Malinowski is history and global studies teacher and academic technologist at the Williston-Northampton in Easthampton, Massachusetts. She is also a doctoral candidate at the University of Massachusetts Amherst focusing on technology integration and the preparation of new teachers.